What Every Teacher Should Know About

Effective Teaching Strategies

What Every Teacher Should Know About ...

DONNA WALKER TILESTON

What Every Teacher
Should Know About
Effective Teaching
Strategies

CORWIN PRESS
A Sage Publications Company
Thousand Oaks, California

For information:

Corwin Press
A Sage Publications Company
2455 Teller Road
Thousand Oaks, California 91320
www.corwinpress.com

Sage Publications Ltd.
6 Bonhill Street
London EC2A 4PU
United Kingdom

Sage Publications India Pvt. Ltd.
B-42, Panchsheel Enclave
Post Box 4109
New Delhi 110 017 India

Printed in the United States of America

Library of Congress Cataloging-in-Publication Data

Tileston, Donna Walker.
What every teacher should know about effective teaching strategies /
Donna Walker Tileston.
    p. cm. — (What every teacher should know about—; 5)
Includes bibliographical references and index.
ISBN 0-7619-3121-X (pbk.)
    1. Effective teaching. I. Title. II. Series.
LB1025.3.T55 2004
371.102—dc21   2003012383

This book is printed on acid-free paper.

04 05 06 07 10 9 8 7 6 5 4 3

Acquisitions Editor:	Faye Zucker
Editorial Assistant:	Stacy Wagner
Production Editor:	Diane S. Foster
Copy Editor:	Kristin Bergstad
Typesetter:	C&M Digitals (P) Ltd.
Proofreader:	Mary Meagher
Indexer:	Will Ragsdale
Cover Designer:	Tracy E. Miller
Production Artist:	Lisa Miller

Contents

About the Author

Donna Walker Tileston, Ed.D., is a veteran teacher of 27 years and the president of Strategic Teaching and Learning, a consulting firm that provides services to schools throughout the United States and Canada. Also an author, Donna's publications include *Strategies for Teaching Differently: On the Block or Not* (Corwin Press, 1998), *Innovative Strategies of the Block Schedule* (Bureau of Education and Research [BER], 1999), and *Ten Best Teaching Practices: How Brain Research, Learning Styles, and Standards Define Teaching Competencies* (Corwin Press, 2000), which has been on Corwin's best-seller list since its first year in print.

Donna received her B.A. from the University of North Texas, her M.A. from East Texas State University, and her Ed.D. from Texas A & M University-Commerce. She may be reached at www.strategicteachinglearning.com or by e-mail at dwtileston@yahoo.com.

Acknowledgments

My sincere thanks go to my Acquisitions Editor, Faye Zucker, for her faith in education and what this information can do to help all children be successful. Without Faye, these books would not have been possible.

I had the best team of editors around: Diane Foster, Stacy Wagner, and Kris Bergstad. You took my words and you gave them power. Thank you.

Thanks to my wonderful Board Chairman at Strategic Teaching and Learning, Dulany Howland: Thank you for sticking with me in the good times and the tough spots. Your expertise and friendship have been invaluable.

To my brother, Mark Walker,
who has provided shelter when I needed it,
encouragement on those days when it was important,
and love always.

Introduction

As we sit at our desks to plan the lessons for the coming week, we often wish we had a crystal ball in which to see which teaching strategies will have the most impact in making our students successful. What teacher has not wished for that special lesson that will cause students to say, "Of course, now I understand!" Through both the research completed in the recent past and the tremendous amount of brain research available to us now, we have a much clearer picture of which teaching strategies seem to have the greatest effect on student learning (and some that don't).

Throughout this book, I will identify teaching strategies that are known to improve our students' learning and understanding when used in the proper format. These strategies should be in every teacher's toolbox because they work with how the brain learns, understands, processes, and recalls both declarative and procedural information. They help students to see, experience, and hear the information clearer and in a sequence that is more brain friendly than some of the tactics we have used in the past. Most important, they are better for students, and that is music to every teacher's ears.

One of the most effective ways that we can teach vocabulary to our students is to introduce the vocabulary, have our students provide their own ideas about what the words mean, and then guide them to examine the meanings in context. Form 0.1 provides the vocabulary that will be examined throughout this book. Look at the words to see which ones are familiar and which are not. Write your own definitions in the middle column, and adjust your thinking as your read through this book.

A Vocabulary Pre-Test is also provided for you. After you have read the book, you will be given a post-test and the solutions to the tests. The Vocabulary Summary offers additional information about these words and other terms associated with motivation.

Form 0.1   Vocabulary List for Effective Teaching Strategies

Vocabulary	Your Definition	Your Revised Definition
Affective modality		
Attention		
Algorithm		
Contextualizing		
Cooperative learning		
Effect size		
Emotion		
Explicit teaching		
Heuristics		
Knowledge domains		
Linguistic modality		
Meaning		
Meta-analysis		
Motivation		
Nonlinguistic organizers		
Pluralizing		
Rehearsal		
Retrieval systems		
Sensory memory		
Teaching strategies		

Vocabulary
Pre-Test

Instructions: Choose the one best answer for each question provided.

1. Mr. Majors provided general directions for his students to create independent projects. Mr. Majors was providing . . .
   A. Heuristics
   B. Algorithms
   C. Effect sizes
   D. Tactics

2. Smell, taste, mental images, and touch are a part of . . .
   A. Linguistic processing
   B. Nonlinguistic processing
   C. Affective processing
   D. Outside processing

3. While teaching her multicultural classroom, Ms. Mosaic often uses stories to help give meaning to the learning. Ms. Mosaic is using a process called . . .
   A. Heuristics
   B. Conceptualizing
   C. Explicit teaching
   D. Indirect teaching

4. The linguistic modality does not include . . .
   A. The declarative network
   B. The procedural network
   C. Smells
   D. Writing

5. Which of the retrieval systems is the most difficult in terms of both storing and retrieving information?
   A. Emotional
   B. Procedural
   C. Automatic
   D. Semantic

6. Which of the following has the highest effect size on student learning?
   A. The cognitive system
   B. The metacognitive system
   C. The self-system
   D. The knowledge system

7. A Mind Map is an example of . . .
   A. A linguistic organizer
   B. Meta-analysis
   C. Heuristics
   D. A nonlinguistic organizer

8. The metacognitive system is not responsible for . . .
   A. Specifying goals for the learning
   B. Specifying the importance of the learning
   C. Monitoring the process
   D. Monitoring accuracy of the process

9. If a teacher wants his students to set and monitor their own goals for learning, he will use information about the . . .
   A. Metacognitive system
   B. Self-system
   C. Cognitive system
   D. Knowledge system

10. If a teacher wants her students to learn the vocabulary related to the lesson, she will use . . .
    A. The knowledge domain
    B. The mental processes domain
    C. The cognitive domain
    D. The psychomotor domain

11. If a teacher wants students to learn a step-by-step process that is used every time they encounter a subject-specific task, the teacher will teach the students the . . .
    A. Tactics
    B. Single rule
    C. Algorithm
    D. Macro-processes

12. Cooperative learning (mark the answer that does not apply) . . .
    A. Means "putting students into groups"
    B. Always involves social skills
    C. Is structured
    D. Requires feedback

13. Which of the following is not a component of cooperative learning?
    A. Positive interdependence
    B. Group processing
    C. Face-to-face interaction
    D. Systemic independence

14. Motivation is controlled by which two systems of the brain?
    A. Self and metacognitive
    B. Cognitive and metacognitive
    C. Sensory and retrieval
    D. Knowledge and cognitive

15. In teaching English language learners, the effective teacher would . . .
    A. Use contextualization
    B. Use pluralization
    C. Use the affective modality
    D. Use all of the above

16. Using the systems of the brain for teaching requires a knowledge of . . .
    A. The hierarchy involved
    B. The meta-analysis
    C. The algorithms
    D. All of the above

17. Explicit teaching . . .
    A. Is involved in both heuristics and algorithms.
    B. Is a part of every lesson
    C. Is not a part of today's classrooms
    D. Is necessary for student understanding

18. Which is not an example of a teaching strategy?
    A. Explicit teaching
    B. Faculty meeting
    C. Modeling
    D. Mind Map

19. Which of the following is not part of the cognitive system?
    A. Analysis
    B. Comprehension
    C. Emotional response
    D. Retrieval of information

20. Linguistic organizers do not include . . .
    A. Mind Maps
    B. Note taking
    C. Outlines
    D. Learning logs

1

Making Good Decisions About Instructional Strategies

Expert teachers generally are comfortable with a wide range of instructional strategies, and they vary them skillfully with the nature of the learning task and learners' needs.

—Berliner, "In Pursuit of the Expert Pedagogue"

Tomlinson (1999) talks about a classroom where the needs of all students are met. She says that in that classroom, teachers use instructional practices "to create classrooms where students have the opportunity to work at a comfortable pace, at an individually challenging degree of difficulty, in a learning mode that is a good match for their learning profiles, and with applications that are personally intriguing."

Much is said about the alignment of curriculum to assessment, but little is written about the alignment of instructional strategies to curriculum and assessment. How can we make informed decisions about how to teach in the most effective way? Once we know the standards, the benchmarks for our subject/grade level, and our own objectives, how do we decide which instructional strategies will make the most difference in student learning? In the past, this has often been a hit-or-miss proposition, but we now have research to make better decisions about how to teach. Ask, "What is it that you want to accomplish with the instruction? Which skills and processes do students need to be able to carry out?" In my book, *What Every Teacher Should Know About Instructional Planning* (2004a), I talk about how to plan lessons around standards—both state standards and teacher standards—identified as objectives. In this book, I will talk about putting together a bag of strategies for teaching that ensures students learn and remember and that is directly aligned with the state and national standards.

Once the standards are identified, teachers develop declarative objectives that state the expectation in terms of what students will know as a result of the learning, and procedural objectives that identify what students will be able to do with the learning. For example, for a lesson in literature on O'Henry's short story, "After Twenty Years," my declarative objectives might look something like this:

Students will know (declarative objectives):

1. The vocabulary associated with the story.

2. The choices available to both characters.

3. The character traits of the two main characters that influenced their decisions.

4. The steps that we go through in making choices.

5. The concept of cause and effect.

6. Ways O'Henry uses suspense effectively.

All of these objectives are factual in nature and are stored in long-term memory in a different pathway than the procedural objectives. Thus, they are taught in a different way than procedural objectives. The procedural objectives for the same lesson might look like this:

Students will be able to (procedural objectives):

1. Develop a graphic model that shows cause and effect.

2. Use a graphic model to determine which choices they would make in the same situation as the main characters.

3. Write a character sketch about one of the characters.

4. Use logic and analysis to determine if the two characters are good friends.

5. Write a second ending to the story.

In the second set of objectives, students must actively do something with the declarative information. They are demonstrating understanding through processes, which are stored in a different pathway of the brain than factual information. Note that students need both types of objectives. Without the declarative objectives, the procedural objectives would be impossible to achieve, and without the procedural objectives, the declarative objectives would lead to shallow learning.

How Do We Implement the Objectives?

The "how" of teaching, then, relies on what the classroom teacher wants to accomplish with the learning. For example, if the purpose of the learning is to help students understand and be able to use vocabulary for a given unit of study, the declarative objectives would be written so that it is clear that students will not only be familiar with the vocabulary words and their meaning but will be able to use those vocabulary words in the context of the unit of study. Research shows that students are more likely to understand vocabulary words

Figure 1.1   Diagram of New Information From Sensory Data to
Long-Term Memory

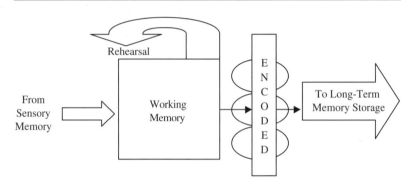

when these are taught using specific techniques. We will look
at both the general categories of teaching and the specific
teaching strategies that help us to reach learner goals.

WHY THE WAY WE TEACH IS IMPORTANT

In order to have a clearer understanding of the thinking
systems—the self-system, the metacognitive system, and the
cognitive system—it is necessary to look at the modalities that
affect the way we teach and the way students learn.

About 99% of all we learn comes to us through the
senses. The brain takes about 15 seconds, or less, to decide
what to pay attention to and what to discard. Approximately
98% of the information coming through the senses is
discarded. That means that 98% of the information going
to your students in the form of words, pictures, smells,
tastes, and touch is lost. No wonder they don't remember!
The illustration Figure 1.1 shows, in a simplistic format,
information coming into the brain.

What happens to this incoming sensory information
during those 15 seconds is critical to how the brain processes
the information and whether it is sent to storage systems
in long-term memory. How we introduce the information,

whether it is deemed to be important, and how we "rehearse" it are important indicators of whether the information will be stored and whether it can be easily accessed when needed. Rehearsal can be rote—that is, simply repeating it or doing it over and over so that it becomes automatic—or it can be active. Active rehearsal involves using the information in some way that is meaningful and useful. Some information and processes are learned better through rote rehearsal, and others are learned best through active rehearsal.

According to Marzano (1992) we should use rote rehearsal when the information will be used in the same format as the rehearsal, for example, multiplication facts. We use active rehearsal when it is important for students to be able to connect the information to other contexts. For example, when studying the Boston Tea Party, we want students to understand the reactions of people when they are not a part of the decision making process. We want them to understand this concept in many settings, not just as it applied to taxes placed on the colonists.

Prior to moving to long-term storage, the sensory information must be processed. There are three modalities responsible for processing the information and sending it to the appropriate storage pathway in long-term memory. This process is important because students may learn information but not be able to retrieve it easily, since it has not been encoded in a way that is appropriate for retrieval. For example, ELLs (English language learners) will have difficulty encoding information in the linguistic modality because they do not have sufficient vocabulary to encode the information into semantic memory, which is the memory pathway that stores words, facts, vocabulary, and so on. For these students the episodic pathway may be more appropriate because it includes context, pictures, and nonlinguistic methods of storage. How learning is processed or encoded determines where it will be stored. The three modalities actively involved in how information is stored are linguistic, nonlinguistic, and affective (Marzano, 1992).

THE LINGUISTIC MODALITY

Most of what is taught in school flows through the linguistic processor, which deals with speech and writing. The linguistic processor encodes this information into networks for storage in the brain. One of these networks is the declarative network, which contains information about events and the information that comes from the events. For example, students are taken on a field trip where a museum docent talks to them about the artifacts within the museum. The information is processed as linguistic, attached to the event of going to the museum.

The second network is the procedural network, which contains information needed to complete a process. For example, a math teacher provides students with the information needed to solve a problem and then gives them a problem to solve.

Think back to the information that was discussed about declarative and procedural objectives. Declarative objectives have to do with the "what" of learning. When those objectives are carried out in the linguistic modality, they are a part of the declarative network. The procedural objectives are carried out in the procedural network. Not all objectives are executed in the linguistic modality; two other examples of modalities follow.

THE NONLINGUISTIC MODALITY

This modality processes the experiences coming into the brain as "mental pictures, olfactory sensations (smell), kinesthetic sensations (touch), auditory sensations (sound), and taste sensations." Using graphic organizers is a powerful way that teachers help students encode information through this modality.

THE AFFECTIVE MODALITY

The affective modality encodes feelings and emotions. It has been said that emotion is the strongest influence on the brain.

Figure 1.2   The Memory Pathways

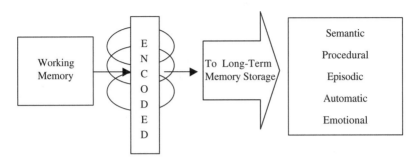

If a teacher adds strong emotion to any aspect of the teaching, students do seem to remember the information much longer. One of the reasons that most of us will remember forever where we were on September 11, 2001, is because of the strong emotional response we had to the event.

So far, we have discussed the sensory data coming into the brain, the fact that it must be rehearsed in some way, and, once rehearsed, how it is encoded for long-term storage. The model in Figure 1.2 shows graphically (in a nonlinguistic format) how the process works.

All information is not stored in the same place in the brain. Current research has revealed five pathways in which all we know is stored. There are probably more, but, to date, five have been identified.

SEMANTIC MEMORY

This memory pathway holds facts, words, and lists. This is the memory pathway used most often in classrooms. It is also the least effective of all of the memory pathways, which is just one more reason why our students have so much difficulty recalling facts and pieces of information. The way this information is rehearsed is critical to storage and retrieval. The information must either be rehearsed repeatedly, or it must be stimulated by associations, by comparisons, or by similarities

(Sprenger, 1999). In order for the information to be processed and stored in this pathway, it must have a connector. The brain asks, "What do I already know that I can connect to the new learning?" This is why it is imperative that teachers introducing a new unit find a way to connect the new learning to something that the students already know. For example, an elementary teacher is introducing a unit on the explorers. Now, elementary students have not been on an expedition searching for new land, nor were they alive during time in which these groups of explorers were living. How, then, can the teacher connect the new learning to prior experiences or learning? She might take the students around the school on a scavenger hunt, looking for specific things or pieces of information. She might discuss this experience in light of what explorers do. She might ask students if they have been on a vacation or trip with their parents to a place they had not been before and discuss the new experiences. There are wonderful books available, such as *If You Had Been on the Mayflower,* that simulate the experience for students. These books could also offer a good beginning activity to build connectors for the brain. The Public Broadcasting System (PBS) Website provides wonderful pictures that can be downloaded to help students "see the learning."

Episodic Memory

This powerful memory system is sometimes called contextual or spatial memory. Just as these names imply, this memory system relies on context or where you learned the information. This is the memory system that allows us to remember events years after they take place—especially if there is a strong emotional response connected to the experience. A course that contains a great deal of semantic information, such as vocabulary, facts, dates, people, and the like, is strengthened by a teacher who uses context to help the learners embed the information in the episodic memory system rather than the semantic. For example, a teacher who teaches a class in which students must learn a great deal of vocabulary can strengthen the memory just by color-coding the vocabulary sheets by topic or chapter. The color-coding gives the vocabulary a context. Building a story around the vocabulary is another way to help students remember the vocabulary. The story gives it context. Students who come to us from poverty, and especially the urban poor, learn best when the information is given a context. Like ELL students, the urban poor often lack the formal speech of the classroom and thus do not have the acquisition skills necessary to store information in a verbal format. A teacher in California who teaches anatomy shared with me how he helps his students build a context for the parts of the body and what they do by wrapping a story around the information. He tells his students a story about a man who gets caught in a snowdrift. He gets out of his car and tries to push it, but it won't budge. The man goes around to the front of the car and tries to pull it. Now, it is more difficult to pull a car than to push it; he is like the pulmonary artery. And so the story goes. He says that since he started using this technique, his students' ability to recall the information has greatly improved. This teacher has taken factual information that is usually stored in the semantic memory system (which is not very efficient at remembering) and given it a context (for procedural memory system, which is much more efficient at recall). Some other strategies to help students remember include:

- Put information up in the room so that it is visible to the learners. More than 80% of the learners in any given classroom are visual learners. Just having the information visible in the classroom helps these learners to remember.

- Give the learning a context through stories, color codes, pictures, music, and symbols. For example, I often use cardboard frames that say "Frames of Reference" when I want students to discuss or review information from different viewpoints. To teach a lesson on environment,

I might place students in groups so that each group has a frame. One frame might say politician, another might say new parent, and so on. Each group would be responsible for looking at environmental issues from the viewpoint of the person or persons they were assigned. The purpose of the frames is to give the information a context. On those days when a student cannot remember the answer to a question, just saying, "Remember it was on the frame for the factory owner" will usually provide the cue to the memory system for accurate recall.

PROCEDURAL MEMORY

Just as the name implies, this memory system deals with procedures or processes that the brain stores in the cerebellum once they become routine. Some examples of procedural memory include driving a car and shooting a basket. Once these processes are learned to the point of routine, we do not need to stop and go through the process in our mind before executing them. This memory deals with things the body does as physical activity.

AUTOMATIC MEMORY

Sometimes called "conditioned response" memory, this memory system is located in the cerebellum. According to Sprenger (1999), this memory system contains decoding skills and multiplication skills but not comprehension skills. It stores the skills that come automatically through repetition and use.

EMOTIONAL MEMORY

Emotional memory is the strongest of the brain's memory systems. Emotion has the power to make the memory stronger or to shut down the other systems. This memory system is in the amygdala, which looks through all incoming information to determine if there is emotion. Margulies and Sylwester (1998) list the following as basic emotions: joy, fear, surprise, sadness, disgust, acceptance, anticipation, and anger. By adding emotion to the learning, the teacher helps to make the memory stronger.

Throughout this book we will examine strategies that help the classroom teacher communicate learning objectives to students. For the purposes of this book, teaching strategies are "best practices" that provide the means and the way to link the systems of thinking to teaching. A teaching strategy might be a graphic organizer, a procedure (such as explicit instruction), or a method (such as cooperative learning).

Good teachers have a variety of teaching strategies at their disposal so they can monitor and adjust the teaching as needed and can reach all students. Using the brain research reported by Sprenger (2002), Tileston (2000), Jensen (1997), and Marzano (1998), teachers can make clearer decisions about how to teach the information before them. Figure 1.3 shows a plan for teaching that follows the way the brain learns and remembers. In the chapters to follow, we will look at each of the components of this plan in terms of implementation.

The base for the learning, called Great Beginnings, includes the establishment of a productive and positive learning climate, the structures in place at the beginning of class, and how the teacher introduces the lesson. This part of the lesson is especially critical because it is at this time that students make important decisions about their attitudes toward the learning. The self-system of the brain decides if the student will become actively involved in the learning and whether the student will have the motivation to begin new tasks. There are specific tactics that we can employ at this time to help activate the brain's natural intrinsic motivation.

The second level of the pyramid involves the declarative information needed in order to process and store the learning. Since factual information is the most difficult for students to

Figure 1.3   Learning Pyramid

retrieve from long-term storage, it is important to teach this information in a format that will help the brain to store and retrieve it more efficiently.

The third level of the pyramid takes place after the factual information (declarative objectives) has been presented. This level of the pyramid deals with the procedural objectives that enhance the ability of the student to use the information in context. The self-system and the metacognitive system of the brain are involved in helping students set personal goals for the learning and in carrying out those goals even in the face of difficulty. The classroom teacher can use specific tactics at this time that will help facilitate this process.

The last level of the pyramid has to do with metacognition or processing and evaluating the learning. This is one of the most important steps of the learning process, yet it is often omitted in our hurried classrooms where we are trying to transmit so much information in a short period of time. By providing metacognition time for our students, we help them to identify what they know, how they know it, and what they can do with the information in a real-world context.

In the chapters that follow we will examine each of the levels of the pyramid and specific teaching strategies or tactics that can be employed to help students be successful from the beginning.

2

Choosing Effective Teaching Strategies for Beginning Activities

N eural science has opened the door to more effective teaching strategies. We know now that certain tools are more effective than others in helping students to acquire and use knowledge in real-world contexts. In Chapter 1, a graphic model of the strategic learning pyramid for teaching that was first introduced in my book *Strategies for Teaching Differently* (Tileston, 1998) was provided. At the base of this pyramid are the pre-learning activities that are critical to gaining our students' attention and in helping to ensure that students will see the relevance of the learning from the beginning (see Figure 2.1).

Figure 2.1   Beginning the Class

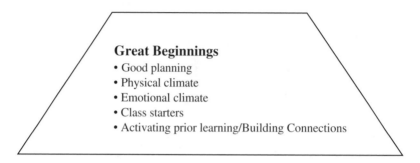

Great Beginnings
- Good planning
- Physical climate
- Emotional climate
- Class starters
- Activating prior learning/Building Connections

GREAT BEGINNINGS

In my books *What Every Teacher Should Know About Instructional Planning* (2004a) and *What Every Teacher Should Know About Student Motivation* (2004d), I talk about the importance of the emotional and physical climates in the classroom. If students do not feel comfortable in the classroom, do not believe that they are accepted, and that they can be successful, the rest of the teaching/learning process will be greatly hampered. Great Beginnings actually begins way before the students enter the room. It begins with thoughtful planning that includes the setup of the room, as well as the planning for positive emotions toward the learning. Since this part of the teaching process is covered in my other books, I will not discuss it in detail here. The list below serves as a summary of the climate aspect of Great Beginnings:

- Stand at the door of your room so that you can see it from the viewpoint of your students. Is the room appealing in terms of color, smell, sound, and interesting things to see and do? We may not have the power to change the color of the room, but we can add to the visual appeal through what is on the walls, the ceiling, the floor, the bulletin board, and more. This applies to both elementary and secondary classrooms. We would probably send the fire marshals of the world into a tizzy if we all began to burn candles in our classrooms to improve the way they smell—but there are some alternatives. Ionized sprays give the room a fresh smell similar to the smell of air after a lightning storm. Those small fragranced cardboard hangers that we often put in our cars also work in the classroom. One of my college students decided to try it in her middle school mathematics classroom. She told me later that when I talked about physical environment in one of my lessons, she was skeptical. She really did not think her middle school students would notice how the room smelled. She bought one of the cinnamon car fragrance cards and hung it in her room. To her surprise, almost every student who entered commented on how good it smelled in the room. Why bother with these small tactics? Because how we feel about the classroom and the learning has a direct effect on the activation of the self-system of the brain. The more comfortable students are in the classroom, the more likely we are to get their attention from the beginning.

- What structures are in place to ensure that students have the opportunity to work together in small groups, in pairs, and as a total group? An effective classroom will make use of cooperative, competitive, and individual activities appropriate to the learning. We know, from brain research, that students 15 and older will listen actively for about 20 minutes before fading off into another world. This means that secondary teachers who rely heavily on a lecture format to teach declarative objectives will hold their students' attention for only 20 minutes at best. For students younger than 15, I use their age as a rule of thumb. If the students are eight years old, I do not talk to them longer than eight minutes before asking them to do something with the learning, or I change the teaching format in some way to break up the reliance on auditory stimuli.

- According to Jensen (1997), at least 87% of the students in any given classroom are visual learners. Classrooms that provide ways for students to "see" the learning are more likely to reach all students than those that rely only on auditory processes. About 98% of all information coming into the brain comes through the senses. Most of us have developed preferences for the way in which we receive information. It is not that we can't receive information in other ways, but that the preferred modality is more comfortable for us. This becomes critical when teaching students who have difficulty understanding incoming information. Jensen (1997) says that if we are going to reach these students, we must re-teach them in their preferred modality. The three modalities most often used in the classroom are visual, auditory, and kinesthetic. An effective classroom provides opportunities for students to hear, see, and touch the information. An effective classroom also provides opportunities for students to discuss the information and for students to move around. Classrooms where there are constant discipline problems may be relying too heavily on auditory methods of teaching. Several years ago, I was involved in restructuring a high school that had many problems, not only with student learning but also with dropouts, with attitude toward school, and with attendance rates. One of the first things we did was to change the way students were being taught. We began to rely more on visual and kinesthetic strategies for teaching. Almost immediately, those nit-picky off-task discipline problems that drive teachers crazy came to a halt. As students were provided opportunities to talk with one another in group and paired activities and as they moved around the room or were actively engaged at their desks, they no longer needed off-task behaviors to break the boredom often found in classrooms where the information is provided either by the teacher or by reading the text. Months after we started the project, I asked one of the math teachers what she considered to be her greatest discipline problem. She thought for a while and then replied, "If I had to identify any problem at all, I guess it would be students who are tardy to first period class." She said she knew that she would not get much sympathy from teachers all over the country who deal with much more difficult problems on a moment-by-moment basis.

- Structures should be in place that not only identify behavior as important but that directly teach and model the behaviors acceptable for the classroom. These structures are taught directly, are assessed, and are reinforced daily.

- The second component of Great Beginnings involves the structures that are in place as students enter the classroom. Before I woke up to the fact that there was a better way to begin class, my students would come into the classroom bringing with them the noise of the hallway. While I was trying to answer individual questions, take up work, talk to students who had been absent, and get my materials ready for the class to begin, my students were off-task from the beginning. Sometimes their behavior even went beyond off-task to yelling or arguments or moving desks. When students walk into my classroom today, class begins. It does not matter that the tardy bell has not rung—class begins as soon as a student enters the room.

I begin class with Mindjogs. These brainteasers may be about the prior lesson, about today's lesson, or they just may be to raise the oxygen level in the brain. The Mindjogs can be on the overhead, the white board, given in advance, or given out as the students enter the room. Sometimes my students work on them in small groups, in pairs, or individually. Occasionally, a Mindjog will be of sufficient difficulty that students work on it all week. There are many books on the market today that address Mindjogs in general and some books that address them by subject area. Several excellent Websites offer ideas for these great icebreakers for the learning. Mindjogs should last only about 5 to 10 minutes. Sometimes I take a grade on them, but most of the time I do not. We found that they help get students into the classroom because we do not allow students to make up the time missed on Mindjogs. My book *Strategies for Teaching Differently* (Tileston, 1998) discusses Mindjogs in detail.

The third aspect of Great Beginnings has to do with the way in which we introduce the lesson to our students. There is overwhelming evidence that this part of the lesson is important if we are to get our students on task and if we are to engage them in the learning. Jensen (1995) refers to this as pre-exposure to the learning. He says that students who seem to be slow in getting the information may just need pre-exposure to lay the foundation for the learning. Donchin (cited in Jensen, 1998) found in his studies that when the brain is introduced to new information, it seems to set the information aside in a buffer zone until the other parts of the puzzle are available. It will then make the connections and bring the information back into activation. If the other puzzle parts do not emerge, the information is simply unconnected and random and thus has no meaning.

The next component of the Great Beginnings portion of the teaching/learning process is called Activating Prior Knowledge. Studies from McREL (Mid-continent Regional Education Laboratory), reported by Marzano (1998), show that activating prior knowledge before beginning a lesson can have a profound effect on student learning. As a matter of fact, if you are teaching in a classroom where students are struggling, just adding this one strategy to your lessons raise the learning level significantly. Jensen (1995) gives the example of attending a new class where the professor immediately begins the new material without any warm up or any mention of making connections to the new learning. By the end of class, he is overwhelmed and worried about the course. Jensen says, "Many learners who should do well in a subject actually underperform because the new material seems irrelevant. Unless connections are made to their prior learning, comprehension and meaning may be dramatically lessened." Teachers activate prior learning when they help students to connect what they already know or have experienced to the new knowledge that they are about to receive. The strength of transfer depends on two factors: "First, the effect of the past learning on the new learning and second, the degree to which the new attached learning will be useful in the future" (Tileston, 2000). We might activate prior learning simply by discussing prerequisite skills to which students were exposed earlier, before the new skills we are about to teach. The degree to which we remember the prior learning will influence our ability to connect the new learning. My first course in statistics was in graduate school, and my class was made up primarily of teachers who were working on advanced degrees. The first night, the professor realized quickly by the blank stares that this group needed a refresher in algebra if he was ever to get past the first lesson with us. Most of us had a poor recall of the algebra that we had taken years before as undergraduates. Because we didn't have a strong prior knowledge, the professor had to go back to rebuild the connections. This also happens in the classroom. All of us have had the experience of introducing new material only to realize that the prior learning is not there. Sometimes we introduce new lessons on subjects for which our students have little if any prior knowledge. When this happens, we must build the learning connection for them. For example, for an interdisciplinary unit on patterns found in snow I would not assume that my students had examined snow except in childlike terms of cold, soft, wet, and fun to play in. They probably will not know that all moisture falling from the sky begins as snow and, depending on the circumstances, may come to us as rain, sleet, ice, snow, and so on. They probably have not examined snowflakes closely enough to know that they are made up of geometric patterns. They will not know that once we understand patterns, we can begin to make accurate predictions. To create a body of knowledge to which the brain can make a connection, I might begin by reading the wonderful book *Snowflake Bentley* (Martin, 1998), about W. A. Bentley, the first person to photograph and study snowflakes in terms of patterns. Or, I might begin by showing my students the pictures of snowflakes taken by W. A. Bentley and published in the book, *Snowflakes in Photographs* (Bentley, 2000).

The last component of Great Beginnings has to do with what we do as teachers to hook our students into the learning. According to Jensen (1997), there are three ways that we hook students into the learning:

1. *Building Connections*—The brain seeks connections. The first thing that the brain seems to do when introduced to new information is to seek out prior experiences or information on which to hook the new information. As discussed earlier, as teachers we can facilitate that by directly including the connection in our introduction. When there is no natural connection, we can create a connection to help make the learning personally meaningful.

2. *Emotion*—Emotion is one of the strongest forces in the brain. It has the power to shut down everything in the face of danger. One of the reasons we have survived as a species is because our brain has a wonderful capacity for fight or flight. Jensen (1997) says, "When the learner's emotions are engaged, the brain codes the content by triggering the release of chemicals that single out and mark the experience as important and meaningful." We want to promote positive emotions with our students, and we do that by adding music to the learning, using suspense, adding costumes, incorporating media into the learning, and a myriad of other strategies. Strong emotion helps us to remember. Therefore, the more we can incorporate strong positive emotion into the learning, the more likely it is that our students will remember the very difficult-to-remember declarative

information. Have you ever been so interested in something that you lost track of time, and when you had to stop working you were disappointed? If so, you probably had a strong positive emotional attachment to what you were doing. You liked it; the learning was probably interesting, intriguing, suspenseful, of personal value, or unique in some way.

3. *Relevance*—Relevance relates not just to making learning meaningful but also to giving it a personal meaning to the learner. How will the declarative information help me to achieve my personal goals, whether they are simply to keep from being cheated on the street to getting into the school of my choice? Jensen (1997) says, "In order for information to be considered relevant, it must relate to something the learner already knows. It must activate a learner's existing neural networks. The more relevance, the greater the meaning." We help give relevance to the learning by asking students to write their own goals or objectives for the learning. For example, a classroom teacher should always provide the state goal and the teacher's objectives for a unit of study to the students and to the parents where appropriate. Students should be made aware that these are the objectives and should refer back to the objectives during the unit of study to evaluate their own learning. In addition, by guiding students to create their own objectives for the learning we are tapping into the need for personal relevance and the monitoring that is taken on by the metacognitive system.

Let's examine the Great Beginnings portion of the teaching/learning process in light of brain research on how we learn, process, and remember. Great Beginnings is directly related to the self-system of thinking, which is the first of the three systems of thinking involved in the learning process. Motivation to begin a lesson, to begin a task, and to pay attention to the learning is all monitored in this powerful system.

THE SELF-SYSTEM

The self-system is composed of attitudes, emotions, and beliefs that are at the heart of intrinsic motivation. This system determines whether a student will pay attention, engage in the tasks, and bring energy to the assignment. Four components make up the self-system, and each is important in the motivation of the learner.

The first component of the self-system is **Importance.** In order for learners to pay attention, they must believe that the knowledge or task is relevant to them and that it is important to know and/or be able to do it. There are many strategies that can be used to help students determine importance of the learning. Here are a few to get you started:

1. Simply tell students why they are learning the information. After all, there are a multitude of concepts and ideas that you could teach your students; why did you choose this particular set of information? If it follows a state goal, tell the students what the state goal is and how you will interpret the goal for their grade and age level. For example, teaching geometry is a common thread or strand that weaves throughout K-12 state goals and curriculums. Geometry at the third-grade level is very different from geometry at the tenth-grade level but just as important.

2. Ask students to compare and contrast what they already know about a subject with what they are about to learn. This will help them to see how the skills build on one another and will help them to realize that they are moving to a new layer of complexity. Form 2.1 shows a sample organizer that might be used to help students think through this activity.

3. Build empathy. Prior to a lesson on short stories, ask students if they have ever had a strong opinion about

Form 2.1   Information Organizer

Prior Information	How Alike	New Information

something with which their friends disagreed? Ask what happened. Did they ever have the opportunity to be proven correct? Did they try to prove their case through emotion, or logic? Read the one-page short story by Mona Gardner, The Dinner Party, taken from an incident in the 1940s in which a woman tries to convince others that women have outgrown the "jumping on a chair at the sight of a mouse" era. You might even add suspense by reading only the first paragraph and asking your students to predict the ending based on what they know so far. Later, after the story is read, ask students to compare what they thought might happen to what actually happened. Ask them to look for clues to the ending.

4. Give the information a real-world context. Tell students how they will use the information in the real world. If you can't provide a way that the information is used in the real world, rethink the lesson. If it is not used in the real world, why are we teaching the information?

5. Create mental confusion. Tap into students' curiosity to know by showing them what they don't know or what they may be confused about. By doing this, we help to give relevance by clearing up the confusion. A strategy that I sometimes use for this is called "Before and

Form 2.2   "Before and After" Sample

Before Learning	After Learning	Statements
		1. Fourteen years before the building of the *Titanic*, a book was written about an unsinkable ship that did not have enough lifeboats aboard when it sank, killing most of its crew and passengers.
		2. At the time of the *Titanic*, people thought it was cool to send messages to their friends in the United States through the switchboard onboard ship.
		3. The night the ship sank, the *Californian* warned the ship's operators of large ice ahead, but the tired operators told the *Californian* to "shut up."
		4. Only people traveling first class were saved when the ship sank.
		5. Robert Ballard found the *Titanic*.
		6. The two radio operators on the *Titanic* were expected to keep the radio going twenty-four hours a day.
		7. The exhaustion of the radio operators contributed to the sinking of the ship.
		8. The *Californian* was less than 20 miles from the *Titanic* when it sank.
		9. The captain of the *Titanic* believed that the ship was unsinkable.

After." For this activity, I provide a linguistic organizer about the topic we will be studying. On the right-hand side are phrases or words from the learning. On the left side are two columns; the first column is labeled "Before." I ask students to look at the words or phrases on the right side and then to write true or false in the column marked Before. Before stands for before learning. After we finish the lesson or unit, I ask the students to go back to the Before and After and again place a "true" or a "false" by each word or phrase—this time in the "After" column. Form 2.2 shows an example of a "Before and After" that I did for the wonderful book *Exploring the Titanic*, by Richard Ballard, who discovered the *Titanic*.

6. The best way to show relevance to students is through our own attitudes, emotions, and body language. When we believe that the learning is exciting and interesting, students are more likely to believe so too. According to Jensen (1997), when we are teaching, our students' brains prioritize the incoming data using our body language as the highest priority; the tone, volume, and tempo of our voice as the second priority; and the content and selection of our words as the last. So, what we say may not be as important as how we say it.

The second component is **Efficacy**. Efficacy is the learners' belief that they can do the task or learn the information. The belief is based, in part, on past experience. Self-efficacy is powerful because it is not based just on good feelings about oneself, but on fact. "I know I can do this because I have had success in math before." This is one of the reasons it is important that students experience success. Success really does breed success. Some ways to foster self-efficacy in our students include:

1. Provide opportunities for all students to be successful—even in incremental steps. Begin with simple tasks and questions and gradually build to more complex tasks and questions.

2. Provide frequent and specific feedback. General, sweeping statements such as "good job" have little effect on student learning. Students need to know how they are doing; they need to know what they are doing right, what needs work, and how they can make the adjustment.

3. Provide ample wait time after questions. Try counting, 1, 100, 2, 100, 3, 100, and so on after asking a question so that you know you are providing the same wait time for all students. There is a tendency in all of us to move on too quickly when we fear that the student does not know the answer.

4. Give credit for partial answers and when part of the answer is correct. Also, give clues when students are stumped.

5. Create a climate where students believe that you are all learners together and that it is OK if you do not know the answer. The important thing is to try.

The third component is **Emotional Response.** Many researchers believe that emotion is the strongest force in the brain. Emotion can literally shut down the higher-level functions of the brain when the learner is under great stress. It can also enhance the learning so that it is remembered with higher clarity. Some ways that we use emotion in the classroom include:

1. *Music*—Bring in sounds of the times for history, sounds of the city for other languages, motivational music, quiet music, celebratory music, and fun music as appropriate. End class with "Happy Trails" or "I've Had the Time of My Life." Kay Toliver of the PBS series *Good Morning, Miss Toliver* sings in her classroom to introduce the lesson. For example, when introducing fractions to her middle school students, Kay Toliver

started the day dressed as a pizza chef singing Italian music. Every time her students eat pizza, hear Italian music, or see a chef's hat, they think of fractions whether they want to or not. The image is embedded.

2. *Costumes*—Kay Toliver always comes to class with some sort of prop. She doesn't do this just to get attention but to help her students embed information into long-term memory. As I said earlier, the memory system that stores declarative information is the least effective of all the memory systems. It must have a connector to the learning; otherwise the information is just so much incoming noise.

3. Use symbols for the learning. Edward deBono wrote a book called *Six Thinking Hats* that is a great model for using symbols and for dividing up the learning. Each of his six hats is a different color and has a specific meaning to the group that is assigned the hat. For example, the yellow hat group might look at an issue from the upside. What are the positives, what can be gained, what are some possible positive results? The red hat group might look at the issue from an emotional aspect. How do I feel about the issue? In my classroom, the hats always have the same role; that is, the red hat is emotional, the yellow hat is upside, the green hat is creative, and so on. That way, after I have used the hats a couple of times, my students know their meaning. I also use picture frames for frames of reference, keys for keys to understanding, and the like. I cut these out of card stock paper (it holds up better) and laminate them so I can use them over time. Because the symbols serve as a connector for factual information, they help my students on those days when they need to remember the learning.

4. Using drama, simulations, Socratic questioning, and student interaction are also ways to use emotion in learning.

Figure 2.2   The Importance of the Self-System in Motivation

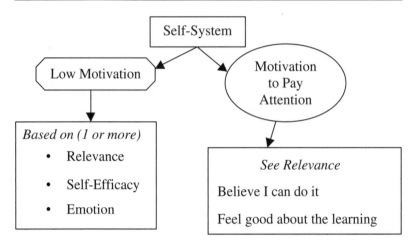

The fourth component of the self-system is **Overall Motivation.** Overall motivation occurs when learners believe the learning is important, when they believe that they can accomplish the task, and when there is a strong positive emotion toward the learning.

Figure 2.2 is a nonlinguistic model that shows the importance of the self-system in motivation.

3

Working With Declarative Information

Teaching for Meaning

The second component of the teaching pyramid is called Information Exchange (Tileston, 1998; see Figure 3.1). It is during this part of the lesson that the declarative objectives are relayed to the learner either by the teacher, by the students themselves, or through media. Declarative objectives are objectives that describe the "what" of teaching. What is it that I want my students to know as a result of this teaching/learning experience?

How we teach declarative information is critical if the information is going to be processed and stored by the students' brains in such a way that it is easily activated on those days when we want our students to remember the learning. We first want to help our students to construct meaning from the declarative information. Unless the new information has

Figure 3.1   Information Exchange

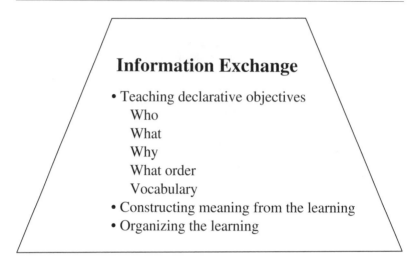

Information Exchange

- Teaching declarative objectives
  Who
  What
  Why
  What order
  Vocabulary
- Constructing meaning from the learning
- Organizing the learning

meaning for the brain, it will be deleted. As a matter of fact, about 98% of all information that comes in through the senses is deleted as unimportant or meaningless.

CONSTRUCTING MEANING FROM DECLARATIVE INFORMATION

Marzano (1992) says, "The driving force behind constructing meaning is using what we already know about a topic to interpret what we are learning. Without prior knowledge with which to interpret new declarative knowledge, nothing makes much sense."

Strategies that help the classroom teacher to determine prior knowledge include:

- Asking questions through discussion or through graphic organizers. For example, the "Before and After" strategy is a good tool to determine whether students have prior knowledge of the subject. Chapter 2 provided an example of "Before and After" for a study of the *Titanic*.

Form 3.1   "We'd Rather" for "After Twenty Years" by O'Henry

Would Do	*Would Not Do*

Instructions: Rank the items on a continuum that goes from the thing you would most likely do to the thing you would least likely do. You are meeting a friend after 20 years and suddenly you realize he is wanted by the law. You are a police officer.

1. Remember an appointment with a friend after 20 years.

2. Pretend to be someone else so that your friend does not recognize you.

3. Turn in a friend who has broken the law.

4. Send someone else to arrest your friend.

5. Arrest your friend yourself.

6. Talk to your friend and let him know that you know he is wanted by the law.

7. Walk away from the situation.

- "We'd Rather" is a strategy popularized by Whisler and Williams (1990) to be used prior to the learning to build empathy and suspense. Form 3.1 shows how this strategy might be used in a secondary classroom prior to the study of the O'Henry's short story "After Twenty Years." On the continuum line, students place the number of the statement where it would fall if they were making the choices. For example, if they would betray a friend

Form 3.2   "We'd Rather" for *The Eleventh Hour* by Graeme Base

Would Do	*Would Not Do*

Instructions: Arrange the activities on the continuum from the things you would do to the things that you would not do. You are having a birthday party with your friends when you find that all of the birthday food is missing. What would you do?

1. Cry

2. Send everyone home

3. Question everyone individually

4. Look for a thief

5. Make more food

who had broken the law, they will place the corresponding number near the "would do" end of the continuum (see Form 3.1).

An elementary example of "We'd Rather" is provided in Form 3.2. For this form, students are about to read the wonderful book *The Eleventh Hour,* by Graeme Base, in which eleven animals celebrate an eleventh birthday with eleven games and eleven kinds of food. While the friends are playing their eleven games, someone eats all the food.

"The important point of any of these strategies is that before exposing students to new content, teachers overtly help each learner tap into his or her prior knowledge and use that knowledge to guide understanding and comprehension" (Marzano, 1992).

ORGANIZING DECLARATIVE INFORMATION

"Organizing involves representing information in a subjective way. It includes identifying what is important and not important and then generating semantic or symbolic representation of that information" (Marzano, 1992). These representations include:

- *Models*—A model of the brain for science or a cylinder for mathematics are examples of physical models. When we use drama, in which students act out parts in a play, story, or from a historical event, we are using physical models of the learning to help students form their own visuals within the brain. Formulas are models, but until learners make the model their own by truly understanding the relationships involved, formulas are not a true representation of the learning. For example, 2 + 2 is a model to an elementary student, but it does not have contextual meaning until the student can visualize two objects plus two objects. Until then, it is just a formula. Visualizing or actually working with two apples plus two apples is a model of the learning.

- *Patterns*—When new information is introduced to our brain, the first thing that the brain does is look for a pattern or previous information on which to hook the new information. We can help the brain to form patterns to give new information more meaning and make it easier to process by using organizers that provide patterns. Patterns are usually either linguistic (relying heavily on words) or nonlinguistic (relying heavily on patterns instead of words). An outline is an example of a linguistic pattern. A mind map is an example of a nonlinguistic pattern. Chapter 5 provides a wide variety of graphic organizers that can be incorporated into the learning for both declarative and procedural objectives.

STORING DECLARATIVE INFORMATION

Since declarative information is the most difficult for the brain to recall (because it must have a connector), it is essential that we present declarative information in a brain-compatible manner. Most of what we teach in school is declarative information, and declarative information is usually stored in the semantic memory system. Let's review that system in light of teaching declarative (factual) information to our students.

USING THE SEMANTIC MEMORY FOR STORING DECLARATIVE INFORMATION

The semantic memory is where all those facts, vocabulary, and words are stored. The problem is that it is the least efficient of all of the memory systems. Try memorizing a long list of useless and meaningless terms and you'll see what I mean. This memory lane is located in the hippocampus. Before this type of information can go to long-term memory, it must be processed in working memory. In working memory it will be repeated and used in some way before going on to long-term memory. Mnemonic devices or peg words may be helpful here, but the best way to handle this information is to use one of the other memory lanes. For example, if I want students to remember the meanings of vocabulary words, I might weave them into a story to give them context. By doing that, I am sending the information to the episodic memory lane, which deals with location-specific information. Here are some other ideas that I have used in the classroom:

- *Visual Organizers*—Nonlinguistic organizers help students to organize information visually. (Approximately 87% of the students in the classroom are visual learners.)
- *Peer Teaching*—This method uses other memory systems, such as episodic and emotional memory.

When we teach something to someone else, we are more likely to remember it. When did you best know the information that you teach? (Probably when you started teaching it—you were practicing the learning.)

- *Summarizing*—Every time we help students put information into a pattern or into a manageable chunk, we are helping them to give it context and to store it in episodic memory.

- *Role-Playing*—This powerful strategy places semantic information into the procedural memory system.

- *Practice*—For factual information to be retrieved from the semantic memory system, it needs to be revisited often and it needs to be practiced.

- *Mnemonic Devices*—Using jingles, acronyms, stories, and so on, is a good way to give context to declarative information and thus move it to episodic memory.

MAKING GOOD CHOICES
FOR DECLARATIVE INFORMATION

Before we can make decisions about which teaching strategy to use, as teachers we must first think through what we want to accomplish with the learning. Declarative objectives provide information to students that they will need in order to carry out procedural tasks like problem solving, model making, and concept attainment. One of the most basic ways that we provide information is through vocabulary. It is also one of the most critical elements and must be covered first, before moving to more complex kinds of information. If students do not understand vocabulary, they will not understand concepts. If they do not understand concepts, we cannot expect them to be able to engage in problem solving.

DECLARATIVE GOALS: VOCABULARY

According to Marzano (1998) and the studies at McREL, one of the best ways to teach vocabulary is first to present students

Form 3.3   Chart to Clarify Information

Word	Description	Draw
Pessimism	To expect the worst	
Racer	One that races	

with a brief explanation of the vocabulary terms and then ask students to describe the terms in their new words and to use nonlinguistic strategies such as pictures or charts to show their interpretation of the meaning of the words. As the students move through the learning, provide opportunities for students to refine their original interpretations.

In order to examine ways that vocabulary might be introduced to students in meaningful ways, look at the following scenario:

Margo Almond wants her students to understand the vocabulary terms that will be a part of their literature lesson.

- Ms. Almond will provide a brief description of each of the *vocabulary* words for her students. She might do this by discussing the words and providing pictures of the word definitions or by showing models of the words (e.g., for words like *cylinder*). She might provide a written description of each word as a handout or part of a booklet for her students. At the elementary level, Ms. Almond might have students make a book on their unit, beginning with definitions. At the secondary level, Ms. Almond might determine in advance how much her students know about the words by asking them to write the words in their notebooks and define what they already know about the words.

- Students might write the definitions in their own words or draw a symbol to help them to understand the meaning. Nonlinguistic organizers are a great way to add meaning to the learning at this level. Form 3.3 is a simple chart that might be used to help students of any age to clarify the information. This is a powerful strategy for helping ELL (English language learner) students understand and store the information in a pathway that is not dependent on language.

- As the lesson is taught, come back to the definitions so that students may revise and refine their understanding.

What did Ms. Almond do?

1. She introduced the vocabulary and gave students a brief explanation.

2. She provided an opportunity for the students to make their own meaning and to put the information into a pattern for learning. In this case, students drew a symbol to help them remember. Other organizers may be used. The point is to show the information in a pattern, such as a nonlinguistic organizer.

3. She came back to the vocabulary as student learning increased to help the students refine and add to their definitions.

Declarative Goals: Facts

Shenequa Brown wants her students to understand the *facts* associated with the Boston Tea Party. In order to help her students remember the facts, Ms. Brown placed her students into cooperative learning groups of four. Within each group, one person represented Samuel Adams, another Governor Hutchinson, another Francis Rotch, and another King George.

Figure 3.2   Mind Map for Boston Tea Party

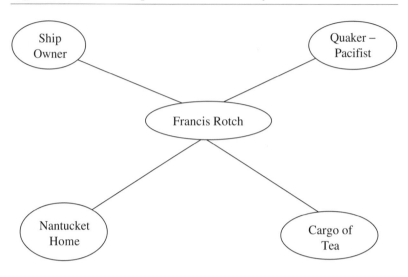

Each participant researched his or her assigned character and wrote a few paragraphs about the character's involvement in the Boston Tea Party.

- Individual participants shared with the members of their group the information about their character (in story form, as if they were the character).

- Individual participants created a Mind Map on their character that was used as they talked about their assigned character in history. Figure 3.2 shows what one of the Mind Maps might have looked like.

What did the teacher do?

1. Students presented the information in a story format (the teacher could also have used an elaborate description).

2. Students put the information into a nonlinguistic format (the teacher could also have used a linguistic format, like notes or an outline.)

Form 3.4   Story Frame for *Piggy Pie*

Chapter _____ takes place _____

_____

_____ is an important character and can

be described as _____

_____ and

_____. In this chapter, the

action starts when _____. Next, she

_____ and

_____.

The chapter ends with _____

_____.

I predict that in the next chapter _____

_____

_____

_____

_____.

Declarative Goals: Using Sequences

If the goal of the learning is to help students understand the timeline or sequence of events, whether it is in a story, a mathematical problem, a science experiment, or a history lesson, organizers (both linguistic and nonlinguistic) provide one of the best ways for students to see the learning. An example of a linguistic organizer is an outline. Students might write their own outlines or they might work from a frame that the teacher provides. For example, an elementary teacher might provide a story frame for students to fill out individually or in groups as they read back over the information provided. Form 3.4 is an example of a frame that might be used for the wonderful book about a witch who goes looking for ingredients to make a piggy pie. The book, titled *Piggie Pie* and published in 1995, is by Margie Palatini and illustrated by Howard Fine. Form 3.5 is an example of a Literature Report Card at the secondary level for the O'Henry short story "After Twenty Years." On the report card, students provide a grade from A to F for the elements provided. This is an example of an organizer at the evaluation level.

DECLARATIVE GOALS: UNDERSTANDING THE ORDER OF EVENTS

Ms. Brown asked her students to put the events of the Boston Tea Party in the order in which they occurred. She could have them do this on a *timeline* or in an outline format like the one below:

1. The financial problems of King George and the English

2. Paying taxes to England

3. Being left out of the decision-making process (taxation without representation).

4. The Stamp Act

5. The Townsend Revenue Acts

6. The rebellion led by Samuel Adams

Figure 3.3 shows a format for putting information into sequence.

Form 3.5   Literature Report Card

LITERATURE REPORT CARD

For _____ *police officer* _____

In _____ *After Twenty Years* _____

SUBJECT	GRADE	COMMENTS
Courageous	D	*He should have talked to his friend first and he should have been the one to arrest him.*
A good friend	F	*A good friend would have tried to talk his friend into surrendering.*
Observant	A	*He recognized his friend after 20 years and from a mug shot.*
Keeps promises	B	*He kept the promise to be there but he didn't meet with his friend until after the arrest.*
Conscientious	B	*He was conscientious about his job but not about being a friend.*

Figure 3.3   Sequencing

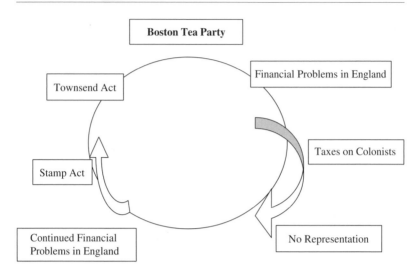

- Next, Ms. Brown asked the students to name other events, both current and in history, in which people felt they were not given a voice in the decisions affecting them. Next, she asked students why it was important to them that they were a part of their own learning and some of the decisions involved in that learning.

What did Ms. Brown do?

1. She led students as they listed the events to be put into sequence.

2. Ms. Brown provided an opportunity for students to sequence the events in either a linguistic or a nonlinguistic format.

3. Ms. Brown led students in a discussion to help them see the connections between this sequence of events and other events. (She could lead them to talk about the domino effect from this information.)

4. Ms. Brown helped students make a personal connection to the learning by asking them how they would feel if they had no say in decisions made about them.

DECLARATIVE GOALS: ORGANIZING DATA OR IDEAS

Marzano (1998) suggests that when the goal is to help students understand concepts, generalizations, and principles, an effective method is first to demonstrate the organizing ideas to students in concrete terms followed by opportunities for students to "apply the concept, generalization or principle to new situations."

DECLARATIVE GOALS: TEACHING DETAILS

When the goal is to help students know and understand details, Marzano (1998) says that the most effective way to do that seems to be to present the details in some form of story or elaborated description first and then ask students to represent their understanding of the details in linguistic (e.g., notes, outline) and non-linguistic (e.g., pictures, semantic maps, charts, etc.) formats.

Mind Maps are often used to help students understand details. Some general rules for using Mind Maps include the following:

1. The center circle should represent the big idea; that is, for a lesson on the meaning of the word *debate,* the big circle would say "debate."

2. Each of the attributes of a debate is placed in outer circles.

3. Each attribute should be written in a different color.

4. Each attribute should not only have the words to describe it but a symbol as well. (By using symbols and different colors we are helping the brain to store the information in a way that makes it easily retrieved. Remember, the semantic memory system is not very reliable unless the information has a connector.)

Figure 3.4   Mind Map on Debates

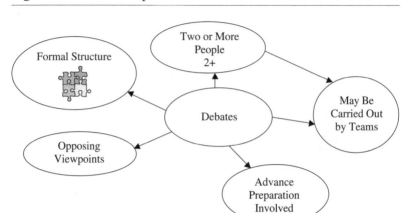

5. Each of the attributes may have attributes of its own as well. These attributes may be connected to other attributes. Mind Maps may be simple or very complex. In my book *What Every Teacher Should Know About Learning, Memory, and the Brain* (Tileston, 2004b), I show Mind Maps that provide avenues for describing systems. Mind Maps like these may be very complex.

6. Mind Maps should show relationships.

Figure 3.4 shows an example of the Mind Map on Debates. Because of the limitation on printed text, the subcategories are not in color.

Lastly, we can make great use of the episodic memory system and the automatic memory system to strengthen declarative information. Here are some ways that we might do that in the classroom.

EPISODIC MEMORY

Also catalogued in the hippocampus, this memory system is strong, especially when emotion is added. The episodic memory system deals with location: Where were you when you learned the information? Where was the information that you learned? For example, was the information on the bulletin board? Prior to a test over material that has been up on a bulletin board or on a whiteboard in the classroom, cover or take down the material. During the test, notice how many students look at the bulletin board or whiteboard to help them remember the learning. By putting the information up visually in your room, you have helped students to trigger this powerful memory system. This is the memory system that helps us remember events in history such as the death of Princess Diana or the attacks on the World Trade Center and the Pentagon on September 11, 2001. We can often remember where we were when an event occurred and who was with us—even if the event took place years ago.

Here are some ways to use this powerful memory system:

- *Bulletin Boards*—Change the bulletin board at the beginning of each unit. Just doing this will help students to remember.

- *Change the Arrangement of the Room*—By changing the arrangement of the room prior to a new unit, you are helping students to put the information in context according to where they were sitting when they learned the information.

- *Change the Student Arrangement*—Change the groups prior to a new unit.

- *Wear Costumes*—Kay Toliver, who made the PBS series *Good Morning Miss Toliver,* uses props and costumes to teach her middle school math class. She might show up in a chef's hat with pizza to introduce fractions to the group.

- *Field Trips*—Well-organized field trips are great if students learn specific information from them. They will remember the learning because of the context of where they were. Unfortunately, many field trips do not have learning goals. Students may thus remember only whom they were with or whom they talked with on the trip if specific learning goals are not set. I like to work with the organizers of the field trips to provide a scavenger hunt for my students in which they must find specific pieces of information on the trip.

- *Color-Code the Units*—Just color-coding each unit or vocabulary sheet will help students remember. Sometimes just prompting by saying, "Remember, it was on the blue vocabulary sheet," is all that is needed to help a student recall the information.

- *Six Thinking Hats*—Edward DeBono has developed a process for dividing information in the classroom. This is a powerful strategy that can be used in any classroom. See his books *Six Thinking Hats* and *Using Six Thinking Hats in the Classroom*.

- *Frames of Reference*—I often give my students cardboard frames that require them to look at information from a different point of view. For example, I might divide my class into cooperative groups, with each group responsible for looking at the learning from the perspective on their frame. For a lesson on pollution, you might ask one group to look at pollution from the viewpoint of a factory owner, another group the viewpoint of a new parent, another the viewpoint of a politician, and so on.

PROCEDURAL MEMORY

Located in the cerebellum, this memory system is related to body movement. Driving a car is an example. When you were learning to drive a car, you were probably very attentive to the mirrors, the gears, and more. You practiced the process until it became second nature. Now, you probably think very little about mirrors or gears when you get into the car. Adding movement to learning activates this memory system, which has unlimited storage and seems to be able to remember forever. Some strategies that I use in this memory system include the following:

- Repetition
- Hands-on activities
- Role-playing
- Debates or Socratic seminars
- Games
- Movement

AUTOMATIC MEMORY

Automatic memory is also housed in the cerebellum. This memory system is thought by some researchers to be the same as procedural memory. This kind of memory is associated with conditioned response. The multiplication tables, the alphabet, and decoding skills are stored here. Some ways to put memory in this lane include:

- Music
- Rhymes
- Flash cards
- Rap
- Jingles

EMOTIONAL MEMORY

Located in the amygdala, this memory system is said to be the most powerful. It can literally shut down the other memory systems. If you don't believe me, next time you loose your keys remember that until you get control of your emotions you probably will not activate the other memory systems to help you find your keys.

Anytime you add emotion to the lessons, you are more likely to have students learn and remember. Marilee Sprenger (2002) suggests that teachers ask themselves the following questions before teaching a lesson:

- Semantic memory content (textbook)—How can I access other lanes?

- Episodic memory content (location)—How can I enhance this memory lane in my classroom through bulletin boards, sensory devices, and the like?
- Automatic memory content (conditioned response)— How can I use music to enhance the learning?
- Procedural memory content (muscle memory)—How can I get my students moving during this unit?
- Emotional memory content (feelings and interest)— How will I use emotions to introduce the learning?

How a student processes declarative information is critical to how it is stored. Processing can be by simply memorization or by doing something with the learning (procedural knowledge). According to Marzano (1992) the weakest strategy for helping students remember the learning is verbal rehearsal. Rote memory techniques such as writing or saying the information over and over seem to have a low effect on student learning and remembering.

Elaboration of the information seems to have a much more positive effect on the learning. Elaboration might be in the form of graphic organizers, or it might simply be doing something with the learning. According to Marzano (1992), all memorization techniques use some form of elaboration. Imagery is one method. Through imagery, students imagine sights, sounds, smells, tastes, and touch. Imagery may be activated through written, spoken, or visual language. For example, a teacher might talk about the sights, smells, sounds, and visuals associated with *Walden Pond*, helping students to visualize the place and time.

4

Procedural Knowledge

Teaching Strategies That work

Once declarative objectives have been taught to our students, we want to provide opportunities for them to demonstrate their understanding through procedures. These procedures were identified prior to the learning as procedural objectives. Procedural objectives are taught in the third rung of the pyramid. Figure 4.1 shows the processes that will be discussed in this chapter.

When teaching for procedural knowledge, we want students to be able to construct models of the learning, to shape the information so that it becomes their own, and to internalize the processes so that they become second nature. In addition, we want students to be able to apply thinking skills that help them to use the processes in a meaningful real-world context. Before students can demonstrate to us that they can use the declarative information, they must be taught specifically how to set goals. According to research by Marzano (1998), goal setting is important if the students are going to carry out the processes assigned and if they are going to carry them out at a quality level. Demonstrate goal setting for your

Figure 4.1   Teaching for Procedural Knowledge

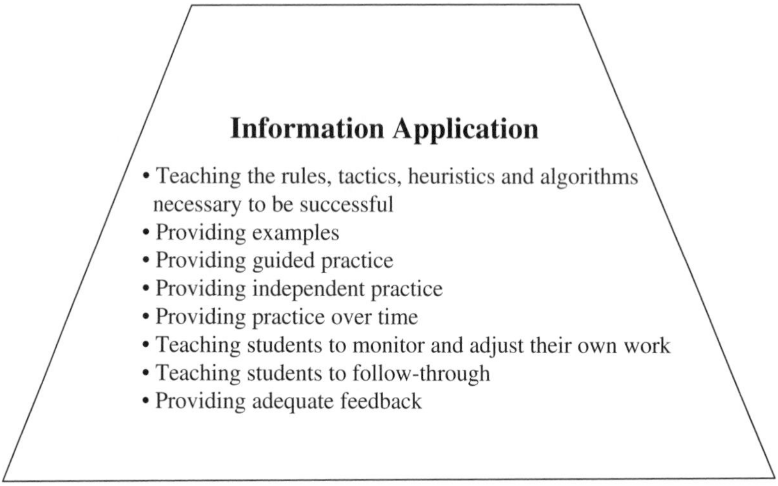

Information Application

- Teaching the rules, tactics, heuristics and algorithms necessary to be successful
- Providing examples
- Providing guided practice
- Providing independent practice
- Providing practice over time
- Teaching students to monitor and adjust their own work
- Teaching students to follow-through
- Providing adequate feedback

students by setting goals for the learning and sharing those goals with the students. Place the learning goals in the room so that all students can see them. In my book *What Every Teacher Should Know About Instructional Planning* (Tileston, 2004a), I discuss in detail how to teach and demonstrate goal setting. For the purposes of this chapter on procedural goals, here are a few ideas for goal setting:

1. Identify the goals that you will be using as you teach, and go over those goals with students.

2. Place the goals in the classroom so that you can refer to them often throughout the learning. By doing this, you are not only modeling good procedures, but you are helping your students to monitor their own progress. For example, if one of your declarative objectives is for students to know and understand the vocabulary involved in the learning, then you will want to take time to show the class that it is important for them to know the vocabulary. Ask them if they believe that they understand the vocabulary adequately enough to proceed to the next step.

Figure 4.2   The Metacognitive System

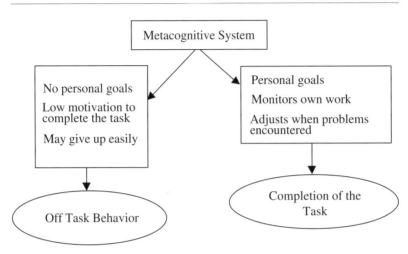

3. Ask students to write personal goals for the lesson or unit. As students work through the processes you are teaching, they may need to change their goals or modify them due to problems encountered or because their understanding of the learning has increased. If you were writing personal goals when you first learned to operate a computer, they would probably be very different from those that you would write now in view of what you have learned. When students are working on a math problem, doing an experiment in science, or working on a project, we want them to be able to adjust their goals when things are not going well or when they encounter problems in the process. If we do not explicitly teach them to do this, they will throw up their hands and quit or turn in shoddy work.

4. Provide students in advance with a rubric or matrix that shows both declarative and procedural expectations. Again, my book, *What Every Teacher Should Know About Student Assessment* (Tileston, 2004c) shows how to do this.

Chart 4.1   Mental Processes

• Mental Processes (Skills)	• Macro-Processes (Processes)
Tactics: Do not have specific steps that have to be followed but general steps or rules. The result is not the same each time; that is, a student reading a graph follows a procedure but not necessarily the same format or sequence each time.	Combinations of skills
Algorithms: Procedures that have specific steps and specific outcomes; for example, if this and this is done, the result will be the same.	
Single Rules: A small set of rules with no accompanying steps; that is, a student might use a single rule for capitalization in correcting a paper. For example, a noun is a proper noun, so the single rule applies.	

5. Use the information on the metacognitive system of the brain to help students perform at an optimum level (see Figure 4.2, page 60).

HELPING STUDENTS CONSTRUCT MODELS

Carrying out procedural objectives involves the mental processes of single rules, algorithms, tactics, and macro-processes. Chart 4.1 shows the mental processes that are involved in procedural knowledge and provides a brief definition of each of these processes.

Chart 4.2   Visual Mental Process

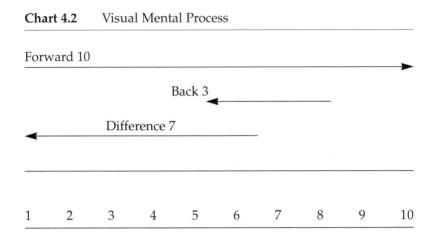

Forward 10

Back 3

Difference 7

1   2   3   4   5   6   7   8   9   10

TEACHING PROCEDURAL KNOWLEDGE THAT REQUIRES ALGORITHMS

Malcolm Walters wants his students to be able to perform *subject specific algorithms*. Algorithms are step-by-step rules that, if carried out correctly, will yield the same kind of results each time they are performed. These are the steps he has taken to ensure that his students can do that:

- Mr. Walters identified the steps necessary in checking subtraction. We check subtraction by adding. In the problem $10 - 3 = 7$, Mr. Walters explained to his students that they need to ask the question, "What do you add to 7 to get 10?" Always add the smaller numbers in the equation to see if you get the larger number.
- Mr. Walters provided opportunities for students to practice the algorithm. He explained to his students that they should set up a rhythm or process that was comfortable for them.
- One of the students added to the process by drawing the process. The drawing looked something like Chart 4.2.

Let's examine what Mr. Walters did to help make his students successful:

Chart 4.3   Sample Math Problem to Determine a Rule

	2	4	6	8
2	4	5	8	
3		7	10	22
4	8			
5				

1. He explained the rule and demonstrated it.

2. He provided opportunities for students to practice the algorithm.

On another day, Mr. Walters wanted his students to perform a *subject specific tactic* (or process). This is what he did:

- Mr. Walters presented his students with the general rules for determining math patterns. For example, patterns in math might be multiples of each other, they might be a numerical sequence, they might be a combination of positive and negative integers, and so on.
- Mr. Walters provided opportunities for his students to practice the learning to determine the mathematical rule. Mr. Walters first provided problems like the one in Chart 4.3 for students to complete and then name the rule. Later, he provided opportunities for students to create their own problems for their fellow students to try to discover the rule.

Let's examine what Mr. Walters did to ensure his students' success. He provided the general rules or heuristics (instead of specific steps). He provided opportunities for students to become familiar with the process. He provided opportunities for students to create their own processes.

Todd Rutgers is a shop teacher who wants his students to be able to perform a *psychomotor skill*. This is how he teaches the skill.

- Mr. Rutgers demonstrates the use of a blowtorch to his students, being careful to provide them with goggles and to review the safety rules.
- Mr. Rutgers asks a student to demonstrate the skill while he watches, making sure that the student follows all of the procedures carefully.
- Mr. Rutgers provides opportunities for all of his students to use the blowtorch and encourages them to find the angle and feel of the strategy that is most comfortable for them.

Again, let's look at what Mr. Rutgers did.

1. He demonstrated the skill and had others demonstrate it as well.

2. He provided opportunities for students to use the skill and find the method that was most comfortable for them.

STRATEGIES TO HELP CONSTRUCT MODELS

Several methods have been successful in helping students to construct mental or physical models for the processes involved in the learning. These include the following:

- Analogizing, which is the process of providing students with an analogy that will help them construct an initial model of an algorithm, tactic, or strategy (see Marzano, 1992).
- Self-talk, which is the process of walking through a problem or process by talking our way through it. Teachers should model this technique by showing students how they use self-talk in making decisions and in solving problems.
- Flowcharts, which are a great way to visually show the steps necessary in a process. The flowchart might show

specific steps such as in an algorithm, or general steps or heuristics as in a tactic.

SHAPING PROCEDURAL KNOWLEDGE

Shaping is one of the most important phases of teaching procedural knowledge, according to Marzano (1992). It is during the shaping phase of the learning that students take the algorithms, tactics, and processes and identify whether they work and how they can create their own methods, thereby making the process their own. During this time, it is critical that the teacher provides specific feedback so that each student can perfect his or her approach to the learning. Feedback should be consistent and specific. Marzano and the studies at MCREL show that specific feedback has a profound effect on student learning (Marzano, 1998).

Guided practice is one of the ways that teachers help students through the shaping process. Vygotsky (1978) hypothesized that "a learner needs the most guidance when working in the zone of development in which she has not yet acquired a skill but has some initial idea of it—in effect, when the learner is shaping a procedure she has been introduced to." Marzano (1992) says that guided practice is the time in which a teacher supervises the learner as she slowly moves through the process. "The job of the expert guide is to help the learner experience possible pitfalls when performing the procedure." Students should not be raced through the process but should be given adequate time to fully understand and practice the process. Students should not be assessed during this practice time except in terms of on-task behavior and following through.

INTERNALIZING PROCEDURAL KNOWLEDGE

The final step in procedural knowledge is to practice the procedure to the point that it can be performed easily and with a minimum of conscious thought. Practice should be massed—that is, a great deal of practice should take place in a short span of time—and it should be reinforced periodically (distributed over time) to ensure that students remember the process.

THE METACOGNITIVE SYSTEM

This system seems to regulate all types of thought that are not regulated by the self-system. It has four functions: goal specification, process monitoring, clarity monitoring, and accuracy monitoring. Let's look at the components of this system. The first component is goal specification. Once students have been given a task, this is the component that builds a goal for the task. Students need to be explicitly taught how to set goals for learning. Setting goals builds motivation to complete the task.

The second component of the metacognitive system is process monitoring. This component deals only with procedural knowledge. Process monitoring checks to see that the algorithms, tactics, or processes being used to carry out the tasks are working effectively.

The third and fourth components of the metacognitive system are monitoring for clarity and accuracy. These components are associated with intelligent behavior, because it is through these two components that the learner carries out the task by adjusting the original goal when needed.

Figure 4.2 shows the importance of the metacognitive system as it works with the self-system to help students not only begin a task but to complete it with high energy.

Figure 4.2   The Metacognitive System

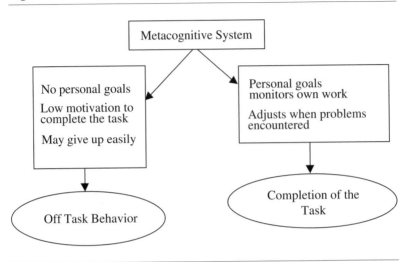

5

Graphic Organizers

Strategies for Thinking

I f we want students to be able to store and retrieve information effectively, some of the best strategies we can use are linguistic and nonlinguistic organizers. The brain likes patterns; in fact, it seeks patterns when it encounters new information. We can help our students learn and remember more efficiently by providing these patterns within our lessons. Marzano (1998) found organizers to be one of the most effective strategies for helping students learn at all levels of the learning process. Organizers provide mental pictures of the learning; they let us guide students to create mental pictures of the learning. One of my colleagues teaches students to add details in writing by asking them to cup their hands on each side of their eyes, as if they were looking through a camera, and has them focus on something in the room to write about. They write in detail about what they see through their camera lens. Gradually, she leads them to describe the entire room by looking through the camera lens as if they were making a movie, one frame at a time.

Form 5.1   KWLH Strategy

Know	Want to Know	Learned	How
Categories 1, 2, 3, 4			

GRAPHIC ORGANIZERS

Graphic organizers are used prior to the learning to help students connect old learning to the new. They are used throughout the learning process to help students understand the learning and to put the information into a format that facilitates processing. Examples of advance organizers that are often used prior to the learning or to introduce a new unit include KWLH, Prediction Trees, Planning Organizers, and Before and After Organizers. Form 5.1 is an example of the KWLH strategy.

This strategy is used to find out what students already know about the new learning. Sometimes I will be so excited about a new unit and will say to my students, "We are going to start a new exciting unit on immigration." My students may groan and say, "We already know all about immigration; we had it last year." That is when I pull out the KWLH strategy, because it not only tells me how much they know but it helps students to know what they know. Many times, I find that they do not know nearly as much as they think they do. On the other hand, if they already have a basic understanding of the topic, that allows me to move to more in-depth studies.

The K stands for Know, "What do you already know about the topic?" My organizer has categories listed at the bottom of the page. After I ask my students to list what they know about the topic—for example, immigration—I then ask them to put the information into categories. I ask them to mark the things they have listed that will fall under the category of political reasons with a 1, transportation issues with a 2, religious reasons with a 3, and so on. I am chunking the information (putting it into manageable chunks) so that they will be able to store and retrieve it easier. The *W* stands for Want to know, "What do you want to know about the topic?" There is always the danger that the students will say "Nothing," so I sometimes replace the W with an N. The *N* stands for Need to know. After we have finished the unit or lesson, we go back to the organizer to write in what the students have learned that they did not know when we began (*L* for Learned) and how they learned it (*H* for How did you learn the information).

A prediction tree is an organizer that is used when we want students to extrapolate data and to be able to distinguish fact from fiction. The prediction tree is used to assist students as they predict the learning. One of my favorite short stories is *The Dinner Party* by Mona Gardner. I use this short story to teach the use of the prediction tree to my students (see Form 5.2). I read a paragraph to my students and ask them to predict (based on what they know at the time) what will happen in the story. They must be able to prove their predictions: "What was said, what was happening, what the theme of the story is, and so on, that makes you believe in your predictions?"

Planning organizers are usually in the format of flowcharts. Parks and Black (1990) use flowcharts to show sequential events, to show processes such as report writing or study skills, to facilitate critical thinking (show arguments, criteria, strength of evidence, and personal values), and for decision making. The flowchart provided in Figure 5.1 is a simple flowchart in which step-by-step processes are shown.

A "Before and After" organizer is used to determine prior knowledge. In the Before column students answer yes or no to the statements provided. The statements should be written so that students' interests are piqued. After the lesson, students

(*Text continues on page 65*)

Form 5.2   Prediction Tree

Final result:	**Proof:**
Prediction four:	**Proof:**
Prediction three:	**Proof:**
Prediction two:	**Proof:**
Prediction one:	**Proof:**

S
U
B
J
E
C
T

Figure 5.1   Flowchart

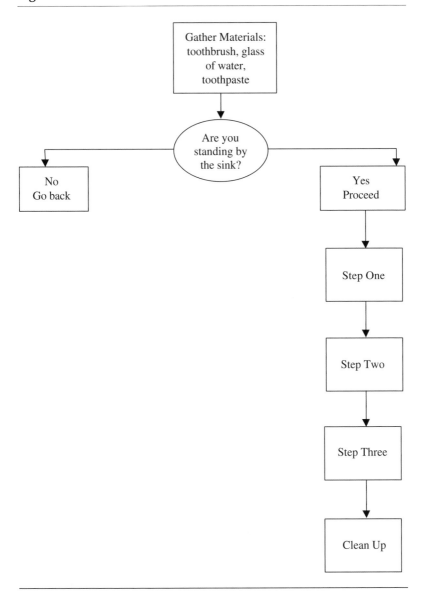

review the statements again in light of what they now know and fill in the After column based on learned information. Form 5.3 is an example of questions that might appear on a "Before and After" organizer on world hunger.

Form 5.3   "Before and After" Organizer on Hunger

Before Learning	After Learning	Statements
		Most children from poverty live in urban areas.
		The United States has fewer hungry people than any other country.
		The United States produces enough food every year to feed every man, woman, and child in the world.
		The major reason that we have hunger in the world is because of laziness.
		Kwashiorkor is swelling in the abdomen due to malnutrition.

1. *Branching Patterns*—According to Marzano (1992), descriptive patterns organize facts or characteristics about specific persons, places, things, and events. Branching patterns are similar to central idea patterns because there is a central idea or thing that is depicted. Branching patterns, however, show not only classes and subclasses, but hierarchical relationships and more complex systems than are usually shown in a web, for example. Branching patterns are a great way to show systems thinking on paper (see Figure 5.2).

Figure 5.2   Branching Pattern

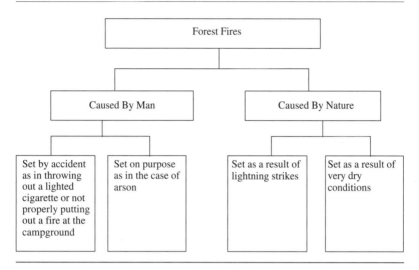

Figure 5.3   Timeline

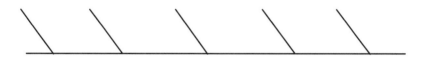

2. *Sequence or Interval Patterns*—These patterns organize information chronologically. Examples include timelines and number lines. Parks and Black (1990) suggest, "Students may use the information on the graphs to interpret trends, correlations, or simultaneous values." Figure 5.3 shows a simple sequence graph for displaying a timeline. Figure 5.4 depicts a way to compare two or more sequence patterns to determine trends.

3. *Process/Cause Patterns*—These patterns place information or events into a causal network so that we can see the sequence of steps or events that lead to the end result. These patterns can show level of importance as well as the order of events. Parks and

(Text continues on page 69)

Figure 5.4   Sequence Pattern

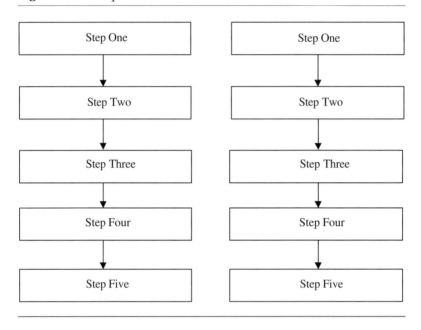

Figure 5.5   Circle Graph

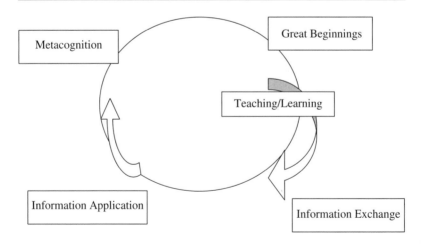

Figure 5.6   Cause and Effect

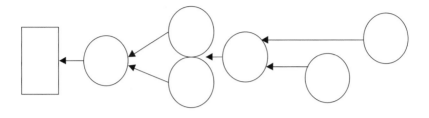

Black call these transitive order graphs. A circle graph is one example of this type of pattern. Figure 5.5 is an example of a circle graph depicting the parts of the teaching and learning process. Figure 5.6 depicts an end result and the events (causes) that lead to the end result.

4. *Problem/Solutions Patterns*—These patterns look at a specific problem and its possible solutions (see Figure 5.7).

5. *Generalization Patterns*—These patterns organize information into a generalization with supporting examples (Marzano, 1992; see also Figure 5.8).

6. *Compare/Contrast Patterns*—These are used to compare and/or contrast two or more people, places, or things. Comparison shows how they are alike, and contrast shows how they are different. These graphic organizers may be very simple, as shown in Form 5.4 where two things are being compared according to a given set of criteria. They may be more complex, as shown in Form 5.5 where more than one concept is being compared in regard to a given set of criteria. At the beginning level, provide students with the criteria for comparison; at a more advanced level, students should be able to set the criteria.

7. *Flowcharts*—These may be used to show sequential events, processes, critical thinking such as arguments,

(Text continues on page 72)

Figure 5.7   Problem and Solution Pattern

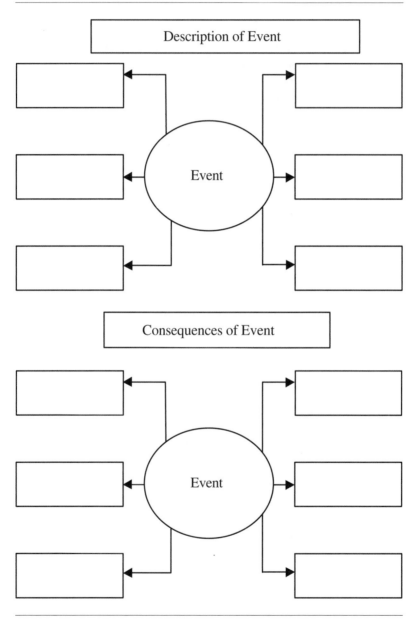

Figure 5.8   Generalizing Pattern

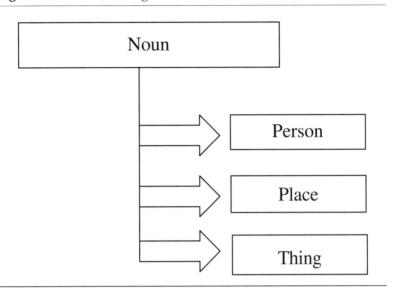

Form 5.4   Graphic Organizer: Compare/Contrast Two Things

Item One: Fact	Factors	Item Two: Opinion
May be stated as positive or negative	How Stated	May be stated as positive or negative
May come from a variety of resources but can be traced back to original source.	Resources	May come from a variety of resources but not necessarily the original source.
Can be proven	Ability to Prove	Cannot be proven
Used for reference, for proving a hypothesis, and for backing up information.	Use	May be used to set up a hypothesis that has not been proven. Is used to back up "I think" and "I feel," not "I know."

Form 5.5   Graphic Organizer: Concept Comparison for More
Than One Concept

Dog	Cat	Attributes	Snake	Frog
		How they breathe		
		Habitat		
		What they eat		

and decision making such as plans. An example of a
flowchart can be found in Chapter 3.

Once students learn to use organizers, they are quite inventive in coming up with their own or in combining organizers
so that they work for them. For ideas on creating and using
organizers, I recommend the following Websites:

www.inspiration.com: This Website allows you to create
your own variations.

www.thinkingmaps.com: Many ideas for the classroom.

6

Using Verbal Strategies in the Classroom

M any of the instructional strategies discussed in this book are visual. I emphasize visual strategies because we know that at least 87% of the learners in any given classroom are visual learners. They need to see the learning before it has meaning for them. As a matter of fact, Jensen (1997) says that these learners will often say, "I see" when they finally understand the information being presented. Graphic organizers are great strategies to help these learners make sense of the learning.

In this chapter, I want to discuss several strategies that are important for students who need and enjoy verbal stimuli in the classroom. The strategies that I will present are brainstorming, questioning, Socratic questioning, Quaker dialogues, and models for thinking and for real-world application of the learning.

BRAINSTORMING

Brainstorming is a great idea for getting many ideas on the table. It can be accomplished with the whole class or with small groups. Prior to beginning the brainstorming, students need to be given a set of rules so that the brainstorming session is successful. Here are the rules that I most often use:

- *Everyone participates*—I want my students to know that this is my expectation.
- *Say what comes to mind*—Sometimes a student has an idea that is pretty off-the-wall, but it may give another student an idea that is viable.
- *No put-downs*—The idea of brainstorming is to get many ideas on the table. At this point we are not looking for quality as much as quantity. If one student says something that sounds crazy and another student tells him so, the chances are that the first student will not provide any more ideas.
- *Piggyback on each other's ideas*—This is one time when it is okay to copy someone else's idea. This is how great ideas are born.

I have an additional rule for myself: Don't stop the brainstorming too soon. The really creative ideas usually come after everyone has gotten the common ideas on the table. For example, if we were brainstorming things that are red, students usually say fire truck, stop sign, nail polish, and so on. After we get rid of the common ideas, we may get things like rage, Red Badge of Courage, and more.

SOCRATIC QUESTIONING

Socratic questioning techniques or seminars provide opportunities for students to use higher-level thinking strategies in regard to the subject matter. When executed well, these activities give students opportunities to provide their own interpretations and viewpoints and to use critical thinking and problem solving. In my classroom, I model the format by taking responsibility for the first of these seminars. After my students understand the tactics involved, I allow them to take over the process. Students, working in small groups, discuss given questions about the learning. Paul (1990) provides the following guidelines for the questions. The type of questions chosen, of course, depends on the subject matter and the objectives for the learning.

1. Questions to clarify. For example, "What do you mean by . . . ?"

2. Questions that probe assumptions. For example, "What is the underlying problem?"

3. Questions that probe reasons and evidence. For example, "What are your reasons for saying that?"

4. Questions about viewpoints or perspectives. For example, "How might that look to a . . . ?"

5. Questions that probe implications and consequences. For example, "What might happen if . . . ?"

For a small-group discussion, a student leader might start a discussion on pollution by asking each member of the group, "Does pollution have different meanings to different people?" (a clarification question).

Next, the student leader might ask, "What are the underlying reasons for different definitions? For example, the definition of pollution to a factory owner, to a politician, to a member of Greenpeace, and to the parents of a new baby?" (a question that probes assumptions).

The leader might also ask, "What are your reasons for your beliefs?" (a question that probes reasons).

Quaker Dialogues

Quaker dialogues are similar to Socratic questioning (questions begin with simple clarification questions and become more complex with time) but are done in a whole group context with the teacher as the facilitator. Everyone sits in a circle.

The teacher begins with a simple question such as, "Where did you get your name?" The teacher answers and then each student, in turn, answers. The questions become more complex with each new question. For example, while teaching an experimental course for secondary students aimed at cutting down on the number of students who make poor choices (such as early pregnancy and drug use), I often used Quaker dialogues so that we could talk about issues and about how we felt about the topics. I will never forget one particular group of students. In this class, I had a football player and his cheerleader girlfriend who was pregnant. They had gotten married their junior year in high school, and he had quit the team to go to work. I had asked the question, "What are things you fear?" When the question came around to the young man in my class, he said something like this:

> When all of you go home each day from school, your biggest worry is what you will do for fun. When I finish school each day, I go to my night job and then I go home and lie awake wondering how I am going to pay for this baby and how I am going to support a family. It is not a matter of love. I love my wife very much. It is fear of the unknown and how I will handle it.

I could not have said anything in that classroom that would have had the same impact as the students hearing firsthand from someone who had been trapped by his choices.

REAL-WORLD APPLICATION OF THE LEARNING

The last rung of the teaching/learning pyramid is an important one if we want our students to remember the learning. It is through the metacognition process and real-world application that we give personal meaning and application to the learning. It is during this time that students reflect on what they have learned, why they have learned it, and what significance it will have for them personally. The process of thinking about the learning may be simple, as in Ticket Out the Door, or it might be more complex, depending on the complexity of the learning. Here are several ideas for how to activate this part of the process.

1. *PMI*—This strategy asks students to provide information under the *P* (for positive) about what they have learned. Sometimes I have my students list things, and sometimes I have them describe the learning. The *M* stands for minus. Under this heading, I ask my students to tell me things that bother them about the unit or things they still do not understand. The *I* stands for interesting. Under the I, I ask my students to tell me if they have anything to add to the learning. This is the place for those "Aha's" that students often have after a unit. I give extra credit for these because I want my students to think creatively.

2. *What, So What, Now What*—Similar to PMI, this strategy asks students to list what they have learned under the *What*. Next, I ask students to tell me why they think we studied the information. *So What* refers to why it is important. The *Now What* is the real-world application. I ask students to tell me ways that the information could be used in the real world.

3. *KWLH*—This strategy is used at the beginning of a lesson to find out what students already know by having them list those things under the *K* for Know. The *W* (or *N*, see Chapter 5) stands for Want to know or Need to know. Students list things they want to find out about in the unit. After the unit is complete, we go back and look at the chart. I say, "Here is what you said you knew about plane figures before we began. Next are the things you said you wanted to find out. Now, tell me what you know now that you did not know when we began [*L* for Learned] and how you learned the information [*H* for How]."

4. *Ticket Out the Door*—This is simply a question or group of questions that I ask students to answer on paper and hand to me as they walk out the door. It is their ticket out of my room. The questions might be as simple as, "Name one thing you learned today and one thing you still do not understand." Sometimes I have students complete the questions in small groups or in pairs. These help me in determining what I did not make clear in the learning. I read these before the next time I have class so that I can discuss the questions that my students have about the learning. For elementary students who do not write yet, I might have a series of faces for them to cut out and glue onto a Ticket Out the Door to show how they feel about the day or the learning in a specific subject. I will have a happy face, a frowning face, and a neutral face.

7

Anatomy
of a Lesson

*A fundamental goal of education is to equip students
with self-regulatory capabilities that enable them to edu-
cate themselves. Self-directedness not only contributes to
success in formal instruction, but also promotes lifelong
learning.*

—Bandura, *Self-Efficacy*

Maria Alvarez is a middle school reading teacher who has
been reading the *What Every Teacher Should Know* books.
She is planning to apply what she has learned to a unit on parts
of speech. Ms. Alvarez knows that all learning begins in the
self-system, where the brain decides if the material is worthy
of attention. To activate this important system of the brain and
to help lead her students to strong internal motivation,
Ms. Alvarez does the following:

- Provides the students with the objectives for the new
  learning. She also posts them in the room so that she
  can refer to them as the students progress through the
  unit. The objectives should be based on the standards

for this unit. By doing this, Ms. Alvarez helps students to activate the first component of the self-system, which is *importance*. The objectives might be written in the format shown in Form 7.1 or in a format that is best for your students. This information should also be shared with parents.

- Ms. Alvarez has created a climate in her classroom that causes students to believe that they can do the work and that her expectations for them are high. Ms. Alvarez has provided opportunities for success for all students by constructive and frequent feedback and by genuinely praising them when it is deserved. Ms. Alvarez knows that the effect of genuine and frequent feedback can make as much as 29 percentile points difference in student learning, according to Marzano (1998). She also knows that building self-efficacy in her students can have as much as a 29-percentile point effect on student learning, according to the same research by Marzano (1998). In Ms. Alvarez's class, it is okay if you do not know the answer. What is not okay is not to put forth the effort to try.

- When appropriate to the learning, Ms. Alvarez will use cooperative learning to help students practice the learning. Ms. Alvarez knows that when this strategy is used correctly, it has a very positive effect on student learning.

- Ms. Alvarez seeks ways to add emotion to the learning because she knows that emotion has a strong connection to motivation and to the work of the self-system. She might use costumes, frames, hats, alphabet soup, or other props to add emotion to the learning. A teacher in my area who has won numerous awards for her inner-city middle school classroom strategies uses a theme each year for teaching writing. This year she has built her lessons around the theme of games. Students have used commercial games and have created their own to help them with the learning. The teacher uses a scooter to "cruise the room" while students are writing.

Form 7.1   Using Standards for Teaching

Standard	*Benchmarks*
Students use grammatical and mechanical conventions in written compositions.	
	1. Uses pronouns in written compositions • Relative • Demonstrative • Personal (possessive, subject, and object) 2. Uses nouns in written compositions • Possessives • Irregular plural nouns 3. Uses verbs in written compositions

We are all more motivated to learn when we have a vested interest in the learning, such as having goals. We pay attention to those things that are unique, like the use of emotion. We are more motivated when we are challenged but not frustrated.

The second part of learning takes place in the metacognitive system. To activate that system, Ms. Alvarez does the following:

- Asks students to set personal goals for the unit. Ms. Alvarez knows that personal goal setting is important to activate the metacognitive system of the brain and to give meaning to the learning. She uses a matrix that looks like the one in Form 7.2.
- Throughout the lesson, Ms. Alvarez will monitor the processes (procedural goals) and will guide students to monitor their own work and adjust accordingly. Ms. Alvarez knows that students are often motivated to begin a task, but may give up when problems are encountered. Ms. Alvarez has taken time to explicitly teach her students how to deal with problems by looking at possible causes and by reframing their goals as needed. She has helped her inner-city students to harness negative emotions and to look for positive ways to deal with problems and adversity instead of giving up. She has helped them to understand that having a plan is one of the first steps in moving through problems. Adjusting the plan as needed is important to completing the process. As a matter of fact, one of the social skills that Ms. Alvarez has taught her students is how to "monitor and adjust." She has also taught them the art of positive self-talk to overcome stumbling blocks. This is important because for many of Ms. Alvarez's inner-city students, the way to deal with adversity has been to call yourself (and others) names and to give up.

Form 7.2   Matrix for Personal Goals

TOPIC: Parts of Speech

PREDICTION: Write what you think will be included in this unit.

GOAL SETTING: Write your personal goals for this unit. What do you need to learn?

1.

2.

3.

The third part of the learning takes place in the cognitive system. Ms. Alvarez knows that this system of the brain deals with declarative and procedural knowledge. She also knows that most of what is taught in school falls into these two categories. In the planning phase of her lesson, Ms. Alvarez wrote declarative (what students will know as a result of this unit) and procedural (what students will be able to do with the information) objectives. Following is a partial list of Ms. Alvarez's goals for this unit:

Declarative Objectives
Students will know:

- The names and uses of the basic parts of speech
- The vocabulary associated with the parts of speech, such as relative, demonstrative, possessive, and so on
- The importance of using appropriate parts of speech in writing and speaking
- When it is appropriate to use each of the parts of speech
- How to identify parts of speech

Procedural Objectives
Students will be able to:

- Use the parts of speech appropriately in written and spoken communication
- Write expressive paragraphs using various parts of speech
- Use the appropriate tense of a verb

To help her students activate the cognitive system, Ms. Alvarez will do the following:

- Build a connection between the new learning and the students' prior experiences or learning (activating prior knowledge). She knows, from the research, that this strategy has a strong effect on student learning (Marzano, 1998). From this book, she knows that there are many ways to activate prior knowledge, including review, simulations, or questioning techniques. For the unit on parts of speech, Ms. Alvarez uses a KWLH strategy. The *K* stands for "What do you Know?" The *W* stands for "What do you want to know?" (this helps students to set personal goals). The *L* is used after the unit to review what students have Learned, and the *H* is used to explain How they learned the new information. Ms. Alvarez uses this strategy for each of the parts of speech the students will be studying: nouns, verbs, adverbs, adjectives, conjunctions, prepositions, and so on.

The KWLH strategy activates the first level of the cognitive system, which is retrieval of information already stored. For an elementary lesson on the book *Snowed In at Pokeweed Public School*, students might be asked to circle the pictures that show what they would do if they were snowed in at school. (In this case, students did not have prior knowledge of the subject so the teacher provided a simulation in which students must make decisions like the ones made by the characters in the book.)

Next, Ms. Alvarez will introduce the vocabulary needed to comprehend the information. Ms. Alvarez knows that one of the best ways to teach vocabulary is to introduce the words through context (as in a story) or by briefly giving students a definition and example of the words and then providing an opportunity for the students to personalize the learning.

Lesson 1 in the unit on Parts of Speech is on nouns and pronouns. Ms. Alvarez placed her students into cooperative learning groups. Each group was given information on nouns and pronouns to read and discuss within the group. Ms. Alvarez used a cooperative learning technique called Numbered Heads Together to see how well the groups had read and discussed the assignment. The rules for this process are:

- Students in each group count off. In this case, Ms. Alvarez had three students in each group, so each group had a person number one, number two, and number three.

- The teacher poses a question and then calls out a number.
- Students who have that number stand.
- The teacher calls randomly on the standing students to answer the question.
- The teacher poses another question and calls out a number.
- The process continues until all questions have been answered.

Ms. Alvarez wants her students to analyze the information on nouns and pronouns. She knows that one of the most effective ways to do this is with nonlinguistic organizers. She also knows that analysis comes through matching, classification, error analysis, generalizing, and specifying. Matching has a high effect size on student learning (Marzano, 1998), so Ms. Alvarez decides to use a graphic model to help her students see the attributes of both nouns and pronouns. Students are asked to make Mind Maps of the attributes of nouns and of pronouns.

Once students have identified attributes, Ms. Alvarez guides students to create Venn diagrams that show how nouns and pronouns are alike and different.

Ms. Alvarez moves her students into using knowledge by providing examples of paragraphs that need nouns or pronouns. Ms. Alvarez provides the tactics or heuristics for making decisions about the nouns and pronouns, including when to capitalize, rules for plurals, and so on. Students work on the assignment as Ms. Alvarez moves around the room providing specific feedback.

GENERAL GUIDELINES FOR LESSONS

In order to determine which instructional strategies to use for a given lesson, teachers must first analyze what their goals are for their students. Is the goal general knowledge, such as understanding vocabulary or details? Are their goals for cognition, such as the ability to generate inferences or to identify how two are more things are alike and different? Are their goals metacognitive (the ability to set goals and see them through with high energy and motivation)? Are their goals based on the self-system (understanding themselves and their abilities)? No matter which type of goal teachers have for their students, research tells us that there are some general teaching strategies that work best for student learning:

1. Prior to the learning, introduce the information in ways that are interesting and that have meaning to the students. Whenever possible, relate the information to student interests. For example, statistics is more interesting when presented as a way to keep pertinent information on sports teams. Learning physics can be exciting when applied to creating amusement park rides. Studying animals can be more interesting to young students when we begin with their own pets or with animals common to the area in which they live. Ask yourself, "What does this have to do with my students' lives?" My favorite math teacher has a sign in her classroom that reads, "I promise I will never teach you anything in this classroom unless I can tell you how it is used in the real world." She teaches higher-level math and her students sometimes challenge her, but she can always show them how it is used.

2. Provide a means for students to hook new information onto what they already know. The brain seeks patterns, so the more we can help create those patterns, the more likely students will hook onto the new learning.

3. Explicitly teach students how to compare and contrast new information with old information. Again, by doing this, the teacher is helping students create patterns and relevance. Both patterns and relevance are critical to learning. Many of the benchmarks for the

state standards require students to know how things are alike and different. Since high stakes tests are written based on the benchmark information, teaching students to effectively use compare and contrast has the potential for raising test scores significantly.

4. Provide students with nonlinguistic as well as linguistic models. By teaching students how to create nonlinguistic models, we help them to find meaning in the information and in the processes involved.

5. Engage students in tasks that provide challenge through experimental inquiry, problem solving, decision making, and investigation (Marzano, 1998).

6. "Provide students with explicit instructional goals and give them explicit and precise feedback relative to how well those goals were met" (Marzano, 1998). Remember that feedback that is general or undeserved has little value on student achievement. Feedback should be given every thirty minutes—it does not always have to be from the teacher. Feedback might be from the student him- or herself (teach students how to use self-talk and other forms of self-evaluation), from peers, or from a combination of sources.

7. Provide praise when students have met the instructional goals. Have celebrations in the classroom when benchmarks are reached.

8. "Have students identify their own instructional goals, develop strategies to obtain their goals, monitor their own progress and thinking relative to those goals" (Marzano, 1998). We know from the study of the brain's metacognitive system that in order for students to be motivated to complete a project, they must have personal goals and they must be able to modify those goals as needed. Otherwise, impulsivity will take over and the student may either quit the project or finish it in a sloppy manner.

9. Guide students to be aware of their own beliefs and interests so that they will be more likely to learn new processes or knowledge.

Through this book I have shared powerful strategies to help you as you teach for long-term memory storage and for effective retrieval from storage. You have strategies that can truly help you to work smarter, not harder. Your knowledge of the brain and the thinking systems of the brain will help you as you work with diverse learners. You know that the key to motivation is in the self-system and that some of the principles must be directly and explicitly taught to students. You have not only learned some vital strategies for the classroom, but you now know the heuristics and tactics for implementing them—and you know which ones are most effective for student learning.

Much time and money are spent each year on the alignment of standards to curriculum and to testing and other assessment instruments. The key factor that has often been left out is the delivery of instructional practices that work. The strategies provided in this book are designed to fill the gap between the written, taught, and tested curriculum.

Vocabulary Summary

Affective Modality

Before information can move from working memory to long-term memory storage, it must be encoded. One of the ways it might be encoded is through the *affective modality*. The brain asks, "Do these data have emotions and/or feelings attached to them?" If so, they are is encoded as affective.

Emotion can make learning so meaningful that it is never forgotten, or it can literally shut down our thinking.

Emotion can have negative effects. Surviving is not just something we do in the presence of a wild beast. Social and learning situations are often survival encounters. When the brain perceives a situation to be threatening, the stress (fight-or-flight) response is activated. Noradrenalin and adrenalin are released, resulting in activation of the gut, heart, blood vessels, lungs, skin, sweat and salivary glands, and mobilization of skeletal muscles. Cortisol is released, resulting in suspension of digestion and the immune system. Under these conditions, emotion is dominant over cognition. The rational/thinking part of the brain becomes less efficient, and learning is often impeded. *The environment must be physically and psychologically safe for optimal learning to occur!*

Emotion can also have a positive effect. Though emotion may impede learning, it also plays an important role in the enhancement of learning. Adrenaline not only activates the stress response, it also stamps with extra vividness the memory of that event.

Anything you do that engages students' emotional/ motivational interest will naturally engage the adrenaline system and result in stronger memories. The bottom line is that information and events are much more likely to be attended to and remembered if they have an emotional component or hook. If the emotion is too strong, however, it can interfere with rational processing and get in the way of learning.

Algorithm

An *algorithm* is a set of rules that applies to a subject-specific task that must be followed exactly in order to achieve a specific result.

For example, algorithms are used in doing math equations, in experiments where a desired result is assigned, in dance when a specific result is expected, and more.

An algorithm differs from a heuristic in that a heuristic is a general set of rules (a guide) to achieve a result. An algorithm is a step-by-step process that must be carried out in exactly the same way each time.

Attention

Since there is no way that the brain can pay conscious attention to all the sensory data that are constantly bombarding it, the brain filters out information that is not relevant.

The primary factors that influence what we pay attention to are:

1. *Relevance*—Information must have personal relevance (How am I going to use this in the real world?) and meaning before students are willing to pay attention to it. Find ways to involve students in the learning by telling them the real-world application up-front, at the beginning of the lesson. Lead them to set personal goals for the learning, and post the objectives for the lesson in the room so that students can measure their learning throughout the lesson.

2. *Emotion*—How we feel about the learning is important. If students do not see the relevance, if they do not believe that they can be successful, or if they are not interested in the topic, it is difficult to get their attention. Use emotion-driven techniques such as music (sounds of the times), laughter (use cartoons and stories), group interaction, and student interest surveys to help create positive emotions.

Contextualizing

Contextualizing occurs when a teacher teaches information in the same context in which students are familiar with the information. This method of teaching is especially important as we teach students from other cultures or the urban poor. Both urban poor and Hispanic children often learn best in a story format, since that is the way their culture teaches information. By placing information into a story format, the teacher is more likely to reach these students. The bottom line is that the teacher must know and understand the culture of the students that he or she is teaching and adapt the learning accordingly.

Cooperative Learning

Cooperative learning is a teaching strategy that enables students to work collaboratively together in structured heterogeneous groups toward a common goal while being held individually accountable.

Explicit Instruction

Explicit instruction is a teaching model that is teacher centered. The goal is to teach new declarative knowledge in the most direct manner possible. The five steps of explicit teaching include:

1. Activating prior knowledge. Build a connection between the new knowledge and previous learning or experiences the students may have had.

2. Presenting and structuring the new content so that it has meaning and relevance. Just standing and lecturing is not explicit teaching and has a low effect size. Students should be actively involved in the learning.

3. Checking for understanding and giving feedback. Feedback that is sincere and constructive has a high effect size on student learning. Feedback that is just "Good job" kinds of comments has a low effect size and may even be detrimental when students know that they have not done good work.

4. Controlled student practice. This is practice in which the teacher monitors step-by-step progress. The mastery rate during this time should be at least 80% mastery.

5. Guided student practice. This is independent practice with the teacher present for feedback and questions. The mastery rate during this time should be at least 85% mastery.

6. Independent student practice. The teacher may or may not be present while the student works independently on the learning. Independent practice should not take place without the controlled and guided practice steps. Sending students out the door with homework on a new concept that they still do not understand is not good teaching. The mastery rate should be at least 90 percent.

7. Distributed practice. The concept should be revisited periodically to ensure students remember the learning.

Heuristics

Heuristics refers to a set of general rules, tactics, and strategies that apply to specific processes or learning activities. Students apply and practice the heuristics with emphasis on how they can improve them for their own use. When teachers provide students with a guide that outlines the components and subcomponents of a process, they are providing students with a heuristic.

Here is an example of heuristics:

Item One	How Alike	Item Two
	How are they different?	
	Attribute one	
	Attribute Two	
	Attribute Three	
	Attribute Four	

Knowledge Domains

Three *knowledge domains* make up all of the information, mental, and psychomotor processes used in learning. Here is a brief outline of the three domains.

1. *The domain of information*—If you are teaching students information, there is a hierarchy that should be used to help them process the information more efficiently and send it to the appropriate memory lane: Vocabulary terms, facts, time and sequence, cause and effect, episodes, and generalizations. Because this is a hierarchy, I would not teach facts until I have taught vocabulary.

2. *The domain of mental processes*—This domain is the "how" of the learning. How will I tackle the problem or use the information learned in the information domain? This mental processes domain also includes a hierarchy that begins with single rules, then algorithms, tactics, and finally macro-processes. If I do not understand algorithms or tactics, I will have difficulty performing macro-processes.

3. *The psychomotor domain*—This domain involves physical processes and skills used by the body. It also has a hierarchy, as any coach can tell you. It begins with dexterity and moves to hand-eye coordination and then to combination skills.

Linguistic Modality

All information in working memory must be encoded to move to long-term memory storage. The *linguistic modality* deals with speech and writing. As data in these formats enter the encoding center, they are encoded as declarative information (facts, words, events) or procedural information (needed to complete a process). Most of the information taught in school is encoded in this modality.

The nonlinguistic modality encodes mental pictures, smells, touch, sounds, and taste. Nonlinguistic organizers help the brain encode information for this modality.

Meaning

Our species has not survived by taking in a lot of information that is meaningless! The brain is a pattern-seeking device. It is always trying to make sense out of its world, continuously trying to determine what is meaningful in what it experiences.

Every encounter with something new requires the brain to fit it into an existing memory category (network of neurons). If we want to make information meaningful to the people we teach, we have two options:

1. Find a way to connect the new information to information that the students already have in long-term memory. The brain likes patterns, and the first thing that it searches for, when there is new information, is a pattern of previous experience to which to connect the new information. This may be as simple as discussing a previous lesson or as complex as associating pizza with fractions. Activating prior knowledge has an effect size of +45. This means that when applied appropriately, using this strategy can raise a student's score from 50th percentile to 95th percentile on the knowledge presented.

2. Help students see how the new learning will help them personally in some way. This may be as simple as

helping them prepare for an exam or as complex as keeping them from being cheated on the street. For example, knowing the fractional parts of a pizza can keep an urban child from being cheated by paying the same price for a slice of pizza that is 1/16 of the pie as others pay for 1/8. Ask yourself, "How is this learning used in the real world?"

Meta-Analysis

Meta-analysis is a study of the comparisons of experimental groups to control groups. The dependent measure is translated into an "effect size." Defined by Glass and others (1981; quoted in Marzano, 1998), the following formula is used:

Experimental Mean – Control Mean

Effect size = Standard Deviation of Control

According to Marzano (1998), "One of the more useful aspects of the effect size metric is that it is standard deviation units and can, therefore, be interpreted as change in the percentile ranking of the 'average' subject in the experimental group." For example, if the effect size of a teaching strategy is .85, that translates to an improvement of 30 percentile points. This means that if the strategy is used correctly and appropriately for the learning, it can take a student from the 50th percentile to the 80th percentile range.

Nonlinguistic Organizers

Nonlinguistic organizers are graphic (pictorial) models that allow the organization of concepts into a framework. Some examples of these organizers follow:

Descriptive patterns are used to organize facts or characteristics about specific persons, places, things, and events. The facts or characteristics need be in no particular order. The

Mind Map strategy is an example of this. Sequence patterns are used to organize events in a specific chronological order. Timelines are an example of this pattern.

Process/cause patterns are used to organize information into a causal network, leading to a specific outcome or into a sequence of steps leading to a specific product. Teachers might use this pattern when the end result is known but they want to analyze how it occurred.

Problem/solution patterns are used to organize information into an identified problem and its possible solutions.

Generalization patterns are used to organize information into a generalization with supporting examples.

Concept patterns, like descriptive patterns, deal with persons, places, things, and events—but not specific persons, places, things, and events. Rather, they represent an entire class or category, and they usually illustrate specific examples and defining characteristics of the concept.

Pluralizing

Pluralizing is the act of using more than one strategy to teach information to students. For example, teachers might directly teach a vocabulary word by providing its definition and examples. They might also provide context for the vocabulary word by telling a story or having students provide stories of the meaning of the word to them. Third, they might have students draw a symbol to help them remember the word. The last example might be used to help students who are English language learners (ELL) and who do not have the vocabulary to give context to the learning. Teachers who provide visual models for them help them to store the information in the contextual pathway (episodic pathway) rather than struggling to store it in the semantic pathway, which is word and fact dominant.

Rehearsal

Rehearsal performs two functions.

1. Maintains information in short-term memory.

2. Provides a mechanism by which we transfer information to long-term memory.

A wide variety of practice activities can be categorized into two major types of rehearsal:

- Rote rehearsal is deliberate, continuous repetition of material in the same form in which it entered sort-term memory.
- Elaborative rehearsal elaborates or integrates information, giving it some kind of sense or meaning such as creating chunks.

Retrieval Systems

There are five *retrieval systems* or memory pathways. Sprenger (2002) says, "There are special lanes for specific types of memory. We need to know how to store memories in each lane and how to retrieve memories from them." Below is a brief explanation of each of these systems or memory lanes.

- *Semantic Memory*—This is where all those facts, vocabulary, and words are stored. The problem is that it is the least efficient of all of the memory systems.
- *Episodic Memory*—This memory system is catalogued in the hippocampus and is strong, especially when emotion is added. This system deals with location: Where were you when you learned the information? Where was the information that you learned? For example, was the information on the bulletin board? Prior to a test over material that has been up on a bulletin board or on a whiteboard in the classroom, cover or take down the material. During the test, notice how many students look at the bulletin board or whiteboard to help them remember the learning. By putting the information up

visually in your room, you have helped students to trigger this powerful memory system. This is the memory system that helps us remember events in history, like the death of Princess Diana or the attacks on the World Trade Center and Pentagon on September 11, 2001. We can often remember where we were when the event occurred and who was with us—even if the event took place years ago.

- *Procedural Memory*—Located in the cerebellum, this memory system is related to movement of the body; for example, driving a car. When you were learning to drive a car you were probably very attentive to the mirrors, the gears, and so on. You practiced the process until it became second nature. Now, you probably think very little about mirrors or gears when you get into the car. Adding movement to learning activates this memory system, which has unlimited storage and seems to be able to remember forever.

- *Automatic Memory*—Also in the cerebellum, this memory system is thought by some researchers to be the same as procedural memory. This memory system is associated with conditioned response. The multiplication tables, the alphabet, and decoding skills are stored here.

- *Emotional Memory*—Located in the amygdala, this memory system is said to be the most powerful. It can literally shut down the other memory systems. If you don't believe me, the next time you lose your keys, remember that until you get control of your emotions, you probably will not activate the other memory systems to help you find your keys.

If you add emotion to the lessons, your students are more likely to learn and remember.

Marilee Sprenger (2002) suggests that teachers ask the following questions before teaching a lesson:

Semantic memory content (textbook): How can I access other lanes?

Episodic memory content (location): How can I enhance this memory lane in my classroom through bulletin boards, sensory devices, and so on?

Automatic memory content (conditioned response): How can I use music to enhance the learning?

Procedural memory content (muscle memory): How can I get my students moving during this unit?

Emotional memory content (feelings and interest): How will I use emotions to introduce the learning?

Self-System

All motivation, as well as all learning, begins in the self-system of the brain.

The *self-system* decides whether to "pay attention" to the information being provided through the senses; it also decides how much energy will be brought to the process. Some of the issues involved in this system to which a teacher must attend include

1. Examining the importance of the task

2. Examining efficacy

3. Examining emotions

Sensory Information

Information enters the brain through the senses (smell, taste, hearing, seeing, touching). If the information is important and/or emotional, it will be processed for the memory pathways in long-term memory. Once the information enters the brain, we have about 15 seconds while the brain decides whether to keep it or to toss it. This is why it is critical for the teacher to let students know why they are learning the material. It is also why it is important to add emotion to the learning when appropriate. Strong emotion helps the brain decide to move the information along to long-term memory.

We discard about 98% of all the sensory information that comes into the brain. We would not want to remember everything that comes in through the senses. Do you want to remember every time a fly buzzes by or a bee swarms near you? These are the kinds of things that build phobias in humans. The downside to all this is that we often do not store information that is important to remember because we do not perceive it as important. For example, you are at a shopping mall walking toward your car when a man rushes by and takes your wallet. You probably will not remember the details around you at the time or the stranger who was walking in the parking lot earlier, because at the time it was not important to remember. Your brain simply discarded the information.

In the classroom, students often miss information that is important to know. Use sensory stimulation to enhance the learning and help students to see the importance of knowing the information. How will the students use the information in the real world? How will it help them to be a better citizen, more productive, or to keep from being cheated?

Vocabulary Post-Test

At the beginning of this book, you were given a vocabulary list and a pre-test on that vocabulary. Below are the post-test and the answer key for the vocabulary assessment.

Instructions: Choose the one best answer for each of the questions provided.

1. Mr. Majors provided general directions for his students to create independent projects. Mr. Majors was providing . . .
   A. Heuristics
   B. Algorithms
   C. Effect sizes
   D. Tactics

2. Smell, taste, mental images, and touch are a part of . . .
   A. Linguistic processing
   B. Nonlinguistic processing
   C. Affective processing
   D. Outside processing

3. While teaching her multicultural classroom, Ms. Mosaic often uses stories to help give meaning to the learning. Ms. Mosaic is using a process called . . .

    A. Heuristics
    B. Conceptualizing
    C. Explicit teaching
    D. Indirect teaching

4. The linguistic modality does not include . . .
    A. The declarative network
    B. The procedural network
    C. Smells
    D. Writing

5. Which of the retrieval systems is the most difficult in terms of both storing and retrieving information?
    A. Emotional
    B. Procedural
    C. Automatic
    D. Semantic

6. Which of the following has the highest effect size on student learning?
    A. The cognitive system
    B. The metacognitive system
    C. The self-system
    D. The knowledge system

7. A Mind Map is an example of . . .
    A. A linguistic organizer
    B. Meta-analysis
    C. Heuristics
    D. A nonlinguistic organizer

8. The metacognitive system is not responsible for . . .
    A. Specifying goals for the learning
    B. Specifying the importance of the learning
    C. Monitoring the process
    D. Monitoring accuracy of the process

9. If a teacher wants his students to set and monitor their own goals for learning, he will use information about the . . .
    A. Metacognitive system

    B. Self–system
    C. Cognitive system
    D. Knowledge system

10. If a teacher wants her students to learn the vocabulary related to the lesson, she will use . . .
    A. The knowledge domain
    B. The mental processes domain
    C. The cognitive domain
    D. The psychomotor domain

11. If a teacher wants students to learn a step-by-step process that is used every time they encounter a subject-specific task, the teacher will teach the students the . . .
    A. Tactics
    B. Single rule
    C. Algorithm
    D. Macro-processes

12. Cooperative learning (mark the answer that does not apply) . . .
    A. Means "putting students into groups"
    B. Always involves social skills
    C. Is structured
    D. Requires feedback

13. Which of the following is not a component of cooperative learning?
    A. Positive interdependence
    B. Group processing
    C. Face-to-face interaction
    D. Systemic independence

14. Motivation is controlled by which two systems of the brain?
    A. Self and metacognitive
    B. Cognitive and metacognitive
    C. Sensory and retrieval
    D. Knowledge and cognitive

15. In teaching English language learners, the effective teacher would . . .
    A. Use contextualization
    B. Use pluralization
    C. Use the affective modality
    D. Use all of the above

16. Using the systems of the brain for teaching requires a knowledge of . . .
    A. The hierarchy involved
    B. The meta-analysis
    C. The algorithms
    D. All of the above

17. Explicit teaching . . .
    A. Is involved in both heuristics and algorithms
    B. Is a part of every lesson
    C. Is not a part of today's classrooms
    D. Is necessary for student understanding

18. Which is not an example of a teaching strategy?
    A. Explicit teaching
    B. Faculty meetings
    C. Modeling
    D. Mind Maps

19. Which of the following is not part of the cognitive system?
    A. Analysis
    B. Comprehension
    C. Emotional response
    D. Retrieval of information

20. Linguistic organizers do not include . . .
    A. Mind Maps
    B. Note taking
    C. Outlines
    D. Learning logs

VOCABULARY POST-TEST ANSWER KEY

1. A		11. C	
2. B		12. A	
3. B		13. D	
4. C		14. A	
5. D		15. D	
6. C		16. D	
7. D		17. A	
8. B		18. B	
9. A		19. C	
10. A		20. A	

References

Bandura, A. (1997). *Self-efficacy: The exercise of control*. New York: Freeman.

Bentley, W. A. (2000). *Snowflakes in photographs*. Mineola, NY: Dover Publications.

Berliner, D. (1986). In pursuit of the expert pedagogue. *Educational Researcher, 15*(7), 5–13.

Jensen, E. (1995). *The learning brain*. Del Mar, CA: The Brain Store.

Jensen, E. (1997). *Completing the puzzle: The brain-compatible approach to learning*. Del Mar, CA: The Brain Store Inc.

Jensen, E. (1998). *Introduction to brain-compatible learning*. Del Mar, CA: The Brain Store. Margulies, N., & Sylwester, R. (1998). *Emotion and learning*. Tucson, AZ: Zephyr.

Margulies, N. & Sylwester, R. (1998). *Emotion and learning*. Tucson, AZ: Zephyr.

Martin, J. B. (1998). *Snowflake Bentley*. Boston: Houghton Mifflin.

Marzano, R. J. (1992). *A different kind of classroom: Teaching with dimensions of learning*. Alexandria, VA: Association for Supervision and Curriculum Development.

Marzano, R. J. (1998). *A theory based meta-analysis of research on instruction*. Aurora, CO: Mid-continent Regional Educational Laboratory (McREL).

Parks, S., & Black, H. (1990). *Organizing thinking: Book II*. Pacific Grove, CA: Critical Thinking Press.

Paul, R. (1990). *Critical thinking: What every person needs to survive in a rapidly changing world*. Rohnert Park, CA: Sonoma University, Center for Critical Thinking and Moral Critique.

Sprenger, M. (1999). *Learning and memory: The brain in action*. Alexandria, VA: Association for Supervision and Curriculum Development.

Sprenger, M. (2002). *Becoming a wiz at brain-based teaching: How to make every year your best year*. Thousand Oaks, CA: Corwin Press.

Tileston, D. W. (1998). *Strategies for teaching differently*. Thousand Oaks, CA: Corwin Press.

Tileston, D. W. (2000). *Ten best teaching practices: How brain research, learning styles, and standards define teaching competencies.* Thousand Oaks, CA: Corwin Press.

Tileston, D. W. (2004a). *What every teacher should know about instructional planning.* Thousand Oaks, CA: Corwin Press.

Tileston, D. W. (2004b). *What every teacher should know about learning, memory, and the brain.* Thousand Oaks, CA: Corwin Press.

Tileston, D. W. (2004c). *What every teacher should know about student assessment.* Thousand Oaks, CA: Corwin Press.

Tileston, D. W. (2004d). *What every teacher should know about student motivation.* Thousand Oaks, CA: Corwin Press.

Tomlinson, C. A. (1999). *The differentiated classroom: Responding to the needs of all learners.* Alexandria, VA: Association of Supervisors and Curriculum Developers (ASCD).

Vygotsky, L. S. (1978). *Thought and language.* Cambridge: MIT Press.

Whisler, N., & Williams, J. (1990). *Literature and cooperative learning: Pathway to literacy.* Sacramento, CA: Literature Co-op.

Index

**CORWIN
PRESS**

The Corwin Press logo—a raven striding across an open book—
represents the happy union of courage and learning. We are a
professional-level publisher of books and journals for K-12 educators,
and we are committed to creating and providing resources that
embody these qualities. Corwin's motto is "Success for All Learners."